FINDING MONEY FOR YOUR SMALL BUSINESS

By: Max Fallek & Kris Solie-Johnson

American Institute of Small Business

7515 Wayzata Blvd, Suite 129
Minneapolis, MN 55426
952-545-7001
Fax: 952-545-7020
www.aisb.biz   info@aisb.biz

FOR REFERENCE

Do Not Take From This Room

While a great deal of care has been taken to provide accurate and current information, the ideas, suggestions, general principles and conclusions presented in this text are subject to local, state and federal laws and regulations, court cases and any revisions of same. The reader is thus urged to consult legal counsel regarding any point of law, or a certified public account regarding any specific accounting implication. This publication should not be used as a substitute for competent legal or accounting advice.

Copyright 2003

Published by: American Institute of Small Business
                    7515 Wayzata Blvd, Suite 129
                    Minneapolis, MN 55426
                    952-545-7001

Printed in the United States of America

Fallek, Max & Solie-Johnson, Kris.
        Finding money for your small business / by Max Fallek & Kris Solie-Johnson
        p. cm.
        Includes index.
        ISBN 0-939069-72-5
1.   Small business – Finance. 2. Entrepreneurship
I.   Title.

Table of Contents

Preface

Finding Money for Your Small Business is a step-by-step guide to help you get the money you need to start up or fuel up your small business. It is written so it can be easily understood, even by people who have no previous business experience. Of course, you may discover some words and ideas that are new to you, but I've tried to explain them in the simplest way possible.

As a hands-on teaching kit *Finding Money for Your Small Business* will show you things to do and things not to do in your search for financing. It will give you real answers to real questions. I've tried to make it a clear and easy-to-understand reference that covers every aspect of finding where the money is and how to use other people's money to arrive at the success you're seeking.

Small business owners usually go into business with knowledge of certain areas and a tremendous lack of information and insight in other areas. Small business owners can't afford the kinds of help available to larger businesses. This book will supply a major part of the financing help you'll need, but there will be times when you will need specialized help, and I'll show you where to get it - sometimes for free.

One problem that faces new and established companies is that of determining true financial needs. Don't think that the more money a company has, the better. Good companies can fail if they have too little money to meet day-to-day costs. A good company can also run into trouble if it has too much financing. The secret is to find the level that will ensure proper operations without burdening your company with too much debt repayment.

Some people make the mistake of finding out how much money is available, then justifying that amount with what is needed to start or run the company. That's why this book goes into some detail about the steps you must follow to avoid that trap, such as:

- Forecasting sales and estimating cost of goods sold and operating expenses.
- Preparing a list of all the equipment your company needs to purchase in order to operate efficiently.
- Estimating expenses for starting a new business or expanding your existing business.
- Preparing a projected income statement.

You'll learn how to convert the projected income statement, startup expenses, and equipment purchases to a cash flow statement that will tell you how much money you need to for efficient, profitable operation of your company.

Then, when you have determined how much money your company needs, I'll indicate what sources are available and how this money can be obtained. In most new companies without enough financial history to prove their ability to repay loans, it is difficult to borrow from traditional sources. I also have provided a description of non-traditional sources for those of you who need to take a more creative approach.

Whatever the source, you will be able to borrow only the amount for which you can demonstrate an ability to repay and for which you can provide adequate collateral to protect the lender. Previous years' financial information plus the projected income statements and projected cash flow statements will help you accomplish that task. In general, lending institutions are willing to lend an amount that can be repaid by your company's income and cash flow.

Are you prepared to lose your savings for the sake of your business? If not, you should probably question your confidence in the venture and your commitment to it. Would you decide against starting up if you knew your chances of staying in business for two years were less than fifty-fifty? These are the actual odds for success and failure in a new business. But not every business starts with the same odds. Those businesses started by people with business experience and expertise have a far greater chance of success, while those started by owners with little or no experience or expertise have a far greater chance of failing.

Like any book, Finding Money for Your Small Business can't do more for you than you are ready and willing to do for yourself. Starting or making more of your own small business requires three things:

1. The desire to take charge of your own future.
2. The willingness to work hard.
3. A practical understanding of how to do the work and organize for success.

Do you have a positive attitude? With all the ups and downs in the business world, an optimistic outlook is a necessity. You have to be able to view each setback as a stepping stone to your eventual success.

Do you plan ahead? Probably the most important ability necessary for business success is planning. Going into business with detailed plans increases the likelihood of business success.

Can you take advice from others? Nobody knows it all or has the time or money to make every mistake on his or her own. Being open to the wisdom and experience of others is the hallmark of a leader. People who listen spend more time doing what works, and less time doing what doesn't.

I have seen small business success happen hundreds of time before. People who have a good idea and a good attitude, and who are willing to act on good advice, have made it in small business. You can do it, too, and I'm here to show you how to get the money that is the lifeblood of all business.

Chapter **1**

Getting Started

So you want to start your own business. Or, you have a business that's "starved" for money to keep it operating or to go to the next level of success. You've learned, or you will soon, that the basic ingredient of any successful business is having proper financing to survive and prosper.

The problem is as simple as this: You open a store, set up a business in your home, or decide you want to build multi-million dollar computers. Before the first customer hands over the first dollar, you have to pay your rent and phone bills, and you have to buy inventory and fixtures. You need funds for living expenses and salaries. It all takes money that you either have already or that you'll have to go out and get. It's the basic challenge every businessperson has to face, not just at the start, but again and again for as long as he or she stays in business.

That's what this book is all about: how to get the money to get going and keep going. I'll take you through what it takes to start a small business. I'll ask some tough questions about you and your competition to arrive at a frank answer about whether you should even go into business for yourself and what your chances for success will be. The next step will be to decide whether you should start a new business, buy one that's already operating or maybe buy into a franchise. Working together, I'll help you decide if your business should be a sole proprietorship, a partnership or a corporation.

I'll help you answer the big question: How much money will you need to not only start your business but also keep it up and running? Finding Money for Your Small Business is intended to get you started on the road to finding the basic sources of money that you should be considering. It covers the difference between equity and debt financing and the kids of loans that are available form banks. Other sources of money to consider include commercial finance companies, venture

1

capital funds, life insurance companies, government, your home, lease financing, trade credit foundations and pension funds.

Equally important, I'll give you some pointers on how to approach lenders and what you'll have to do to convince them you're a good risk. By the time you finish reading this book, you should have a firm idea of whether you have to finance it, how to prepare a loan proposal and where to go fro the money you will need.

IF YOU ALREADY OWN A SMALL BUSINESS

As a small business owner you don't have to be reminded of the money difficulties that can arise, usually at the most unexpected times. You know all the costs of operating a business, such items as:

- Salaries
- Materials
- Depreciation
- Technology
- Advertising
- Insurance
- Utilities

- Rent
- Taxes
- Interest on loans
- Professional services
- Working capital
- Miscellaneous Costs

There are always demands on your bankroll, and if income doesn't meet them you have to find someone who can protect you from the wolf at the door.

Something like this may have happened to you or someone you know: Tom Reilly is a successful businessman who has a well-established mail order business. For years he has depended on a weekly mailbox full of checks to pay the twice-monthly salaries his five employees and himself. One Monday the mail was unexpectedly light, and the checks he expected are nowhere in sight. If he doesn't take some fast action, he'll have to dig into his savings or get the money elsewhere to meet the payroll. Fortunately, Tom had built up a good relationship with his banker over the eight years he had been in business. He pays a visit to the bank and, because of his established good record, got a loan on the spot.

Any kind of business, new or established is in constant need of money. If sales keep up and customers pay their bills, things run smoothly. If sales keep up and customers pay their bills, things run smoothly. When that doesn't happen - and there are countless ways for things to go wrong - money is the usual remedy.

IF YOU ARE STARTING A SMALL BUSINESS

When starting a new business, there are three important factors to consider: the idea, the need for your product or service, and the type of competitors you will face.

2

The Idea

Every business venture is based on an idea. If your idea involves a product, will you manufacture, subcontract, assemble or buy it? Will it be more suitable for retail or mail order? Does it require a sales staff or distributors? If it's new product, will you need a model, patent, or copyright? If it's an existing product, what makes your product better than others?

If your idea is for a service, can it be handled by you or will it require other personnel? Are special skills or equipment, or both, required? If you don't have the skills, are they available through employees? Can the service be organized and marketed? Is it a new service or an improvement of an existing service?
If your idea is for a retail establishment, will it be something new or competitive? Will location be its primary asset? What will set it apart from other retailers? Will the adjacent stores create the type of traffic you desire?

The Need

Is there a real need for what you have to offer? Does a market exist, and is it reasonably large enough for you to enter? Will there be opportunity for future growth? Where are the buyers who need your product or service - in industry or in the consumer marketplace? Are there any other restrictions to your market: age disposable income level, geography, or season? Will you have to create a market?

The Competition

Regardless of whether your product or service is new or already on the market, who or what are your competitors? Are they direct competition? Are they well established and able to withstand your efforts? Where are the competitors' marketing areas? If direct competition exists, how does your offering stack up in terms of quality, price, or benefits? If it's a new product, is it easy to duplicate? Will you be able to protect it?

PLAN FOR THE BEST AND PROTECT YOURSELF AGAINST THE WORST

How often do we hear stories about people and companies having to close or enter bankruptcy? And why is it that we keep hearing nine out of ten new businesses will fail or close within two years?
Any number of reasons that can explain why businesses flop:

- Low sales volume
- Insufficient capital
- Wrong location
- Incorrect merchandise
- Competition that is too strong
- Ineffective advertising
- Changing market conditions
- Poor management
- Lack of know how

If you want to go into business and want the best chance of making a go of it, there is something you can do: Prepare for the best and protect yourself against the worst.

You can plan ahead. It's no mystery. I have helped a lot of businesses get going and stay successful. I also have seen many enterprises fail because owners didn't take good advice from people who already knew what they needed to know about how business really works. We could write a book, and this is it, that has the kind of facts every business owner should have to get the maximum chance for success. Successful business owners are those who don't try to reinvent the wheel, have wisely taken good counsel, done it right, and come out on top.

One thing is for sure: Anybody who runs any business bigger than a lemonade stand will find out quickly that the most efficient way to get seed money or financing for your business is to write a plan. Banks, venture capitalists, private investors, even smart friends, and relatives insist on it. Even if you could get all the start-up money you need, without having a plan, you're only fooling yourself. The woods are full of people who went into business with just a good idea and an expectation of steady sales, only to end up in bankruptcy court. The court will insist you work up a plan, only then it will be called a reorganization plan.

Whether you write out a few pages of notes or prepare a well-thought-out and carefully detailed document, you will need to know where you are, where you're going and where you can expect to be. Here's the payoff: the most important reason to plan ahead is that you'll discover how you can manage your business more profitably. The truth is, planning will not ensure your success. But nothing will give you a greater chance of success than preparing a carefully crafted plan and following it.

CHARACTERISTICS OF A SUCCESSFUL SMALL BUSINESS OPERATOR

This great country is indeed the "land of opportunity." Nowhere else in the world can you control your destiny as completely as you can if you're fortunate enough to be living in the United States. Every time we sing "the Star Spangled Banner" we are reminded that our country is the "land of the free and the home of the brave." In most cases, however, too few are brave enough to venture out on the road to freedom. For those of us who have made this venture, however, few would choose to go back.

Success in small business is not a matter left to chance or change. We have all heard of successful entrepreneurs who were lucky or in the right place at the right time. Luck or good timing is not something you can count on, nor will it carry you through years of operating a business successfully. Furthermore, successful small business operators, really make their own breaks or luck, or put themselves in the right place at the right time.

American small business operators number in the millions. Of the approximately 25 million businesses in this country, more than 15 million are operated as sole proprietorships; in other words, most small businesses in America are run by people who are in business for themselves.

Who are these people we call successful small business operators? While there are no absolutes, we can make some general observations about them:

1. They *love to make money*. Some enjoy the things that money can buy; others view money as just a way of measuring success; still others see money as power, financial security, or means of positive self-esteem.
2. They have *bigger dreams* than most other people. They challenge themselves to do more because they want more - more of the money, freedom and status that accompany small business ownership.
3. Successful small business owners are intensely *success oriented*. They have a need - sometimes a burning desire - to succeed. They need to prove themselves, to their friends and acquaintances, to their families, and to their toughest critics - themselves.
4. Small business owners *work harder* than most people. Some even think working 18 hours a day is fun. They don't mind putting in extra effort with the prospect of reaping the rewards. Successful people do not like to work hard so someone else can reap the rewards. Maybe that's why, as a group, they don't like working for other people.
5. Small Business Owners are *better at something* than most people. Some have outstanding artistic talent; others are brilliant marketers; still others have a natural gift for organizing; and most are born leaders. They have something extra that will help us succeed, and they are smart enough to make the most of it.
6. Successful small business operators *look at risks differently* than most people do. They understand the basic risk and reward ratio of life: the greater the risks, the greater the rewards. In other words, no guts, no glory. They accept the fact that they can't win if they're not in the game. But their risks are almost always carefully calculated and supported by confidence and belief in themselves. They reduce the risk by learning the odds and knowing what they're doing.

7. Small business owners are *proud of their abilities* and their achievements. Their success proves that they are not average or mediocre. Success gives them great satisfaction -- and pride!

ARE YOU READY?

Even before you think about what goes into your planning, think about your needs and desires. Operating a business is a lot different than checking into work in the morning, doing a job and collecting a paycheck at the end of the week. Make no mistake, operating a business is hard work, with long hours and lots of complications: from quality control, to hiring and managing people, to keeping up a constant cash flow. And if you're the right kind of person, you'll thrive on it.

I know from years of working in the field and studies of successful entrepreneurs that business ownership attracts certain kinds of people. If you fit the profile, you probably have the right stuff to go out on your own. If you don't, you will want to think about developing some of these traits:

- Initiative, the first and most important quality
- Independence and a healthy ego
- Desire to maintain firm control over your future
- Organizational ability to get others to work with you
- Drive and enthusiasm
- Emotional stability for tough times and for success
- Self-confidence, with high standards for yourself and others
- Willingness to learn new things and sacrifice for success
- Willingness to take calculated risks
- Good communication abilities
- A sense of humor

Without these characteristics, it's back to the drawing board. Obviously any of these personality traits is a mix of positive and negative qualities. The same kind of hard driving personality that generates the creative energy to start a business can also destroy it. The trick is to know yourself and know how to channel the best of what you've got.

If you reflect most of the good qualities in the preceding list you are the kind of person who will have the best chance to build a business and reap its rewards. You will also know some of the reasons why otherwise capable businesspeople fail. What makes some businesses successful will be one of the most important things you'll learn in this book.

GET STARTED!

There are only two things you can be sure of about going into business: One is that you will be going into partnership with the government - it may have a lot to say about how you conduct your business and will certainly have a hand in your profits; the other thing you can count on is change.

You already have much of the information you need. You've probably been thinking about going into business or developing your business for months or years. You have been gathering fragments of information and planning what you'll do when you get going. The idea looks good or you wouldn't have gotten as far as buying this book. The time has come to get it out of your mind or off the scraps of paper you've collected and put it together into a blueprint that leads you to action.

Here's one important hint about what it really takes to make it in business: The quality of management and the quality of marketing are the two most essential factors, and they begin with knowing yourself and your business. What about financing? Though it's important, management and marketing will go a long way to determining how you get the capital you need.

In the next section you will learn about the first step in planning; what kind of business is best for you and whether you should start up fresh, buy an existing business or look into franchising.

CHAPTER 2

Starting up, Buying or Franchising

Think about this: an average of 500,000 new businesses have been started in the United States every year over the past ten years. That's a lot of competition. But every year many thousands of men and women start the same way, and succeed, with just an idea and a little money they've begged, borrowed or dug out of their savings.

Being in charge of your own business does not necessarily mean starting from scratch. It does not mean having to do it the hard or slow way. If you have some money to begin with or can convince a few friends or relatives to pitch in, it may be to your advantage to buy an existing business. It's like finding your dream house: You can build it from scratch, or you can wait until you come across the right one and buy it. In the first case, it's a little harder on your nerves. In the second case, harder on your pocketbook. Take your pick. A third option is franchising, which minimizes your risk, since you're offering a proven product and have the support of franchiser services.

STARTING UP

Figure 2.1 summarizes the advantages and disadvantages of the start-up option for small business. Take the case of Jeffrey Anderson, who had put in 15 years at a large management consultation firm in upstate New York. He generally liked his job, but had become dissatisfied. It was the same grind every day, and he was getting bored. From time to time he considered going into business for himself, but never really got active until he came up with a business idea that appealed to his considerable interest in music. The idea was to open a record store, but one with a difference, offering a 20 percent discount for customers who would join his club and agree to buy at least ten records a year.

Figure 2.1 Start-up business

Advantages:	*Disadvantages:*
<ul><li>Fulfills the desire for complete business independence</li><li>Freedom to establish your preferred location</li><li>Choice of suppliers, sources and employees</li><li>Create your own customer target profile</li><li>Redecoration or enlargement to fit your own needs</li><li>New equipment, fixtures and leases</li><li>Fresh supplies, inventory and materials</li><li>No royalties to pay to a franchiser</li><li>No franchisor or seller to tell you how you run your business.</li></ul>	<ul><li>You must provide all the capital</li><li>Potential competitors may present problems</li><li>Harder to estimate how much it will cost to get into business</li><li>No past history of return on your investment</li><li>Maximum of risk and investment</li><li>On your own in site location, training, financing, marketing, promotion, and record keeping</li><li>Most new ventures require a few years of intensive effort before profits start rolling in</li></ul>

Anderson did some research into the retail record business and decided that, despite the heavy local competition, he had a good chance of success with his discount idea. Anderson rented a 2,000-square-foot storefront in the downtown business section and secured a $45,000 loan through the Small Business Administration.

From the beginning he was faced with two problems: competing in a crowded market and bringing in enough money to make up for the discounts he gave on his records. There were a few years when he had to hang on by his fingernails. But with a basically good idea and persistence, Anderson was able to make a go of it in a business he really enjoyed, despite his long working hours. Today, thanks to a unique idea and careful attention to customer wants, an enlarged Anderson's Music Shop sells more recordings than any of his competitors in the marketing area.

Unquestionably there are opportunities for new businesses to succeed in the marketplace. Anderson found a position in the business world and made good by providing customers with a product and service they wanted. This attention to the customer is at the core of most successful businesses.

Product, service and profit are three vital ingredients for running a successful business, but they can also be used to decide what business to get into. Prospective business owners too often choose a business simply because it seems like fun or easy, without thinking about whether the business will meet customer demand. At the same time, attention must be given to the need for profitable sales volume. Without customer demand, there are too few sales, and without sales, no business can succeed.

Top New Businesses

Business ideas are created from countless sources: hobbies, market gaps, and technological advances and others. According to government statistics, some of the most popular and successful new business areas include:

- Accounting services
- Auto parts
- Automobile/truck rental service
- Car washes
- Carpet cleaning
- Convenience stores
- Copying establishments
- Diet services
- Draperies
- Employment placement services
- Fast food
- Car care centers
- Hair care
- Laundry and dry cleaning services
- Lawn care
- Leisure and travel
- Muffler replacement
- Picture frames
- Pre-school and school age educational services
- Printing
- Real estate outlets
- Retail tire outlets
- Sewer and drain cleaning
- Tax preparation
- Transmission shops

From Entrepreneur Magazine's 4th Annual Million Dollar Ideas from January 2003, here are the businesses they believe are the next HOT businesses:

- Auto Accessories
- EBay related products
- Instant Messaging
- Maternity Clothes
- Online Gaming
- Pet Products
- Bed & Breakfast
- Home Entertainment Installation
- Kiosks
- Niche Dating Services
- Online Learning

11

And these are just a few of the kinds of businesses that people are starting every day. When you decide to start a business, make sure it's right for you. Be careful to find out if you really have the skills necessary to run the venture you've chosen. The more background you have in a particular business, the more likely you are to succeed. While some people have an inherent ability to succeed in whatever business they try, most of us find it wiser to stick to something we know. Starting or running your own business is a difficult, time-consuming undertaking. You lessen the risk of failure if you bring some experience into the mix.

The following are some of the questions you must ask yourself in the earliest stages of your business development:

- Is your product or service new or established?
- Do you have skills or experience that relate?
- What size of business can you handle?
- Do you intend to go it alone? With employees?
- Is there a preferred or ideal location?
- How much of your own capital is available?
- How much additional capital can you raise?
- Are partners being considered? For capital? For helpful skills?
- Are you going to run the business on a part-time or full-time basis?

Every business and businessperson has limitations and every business has just so much financing available. It's best to know at the outset what you can handle and how many problems you can juggle at one time.

Can You Handle the Investment?

The desire to go into business is one thing; the most important financial consideration is the minimum amount of capital required. This is what it will cost you to get the business started and keep it running for at least one year. For the small businessperson, the less expensive an operation is, the more realistic a prospect it becomes.

In the next chapter, we will discuss the Five Money Keys for business success. Money Key #5 states: The successful small businessperson knows how to find and use someone else's money in order to make money! This is particularly true if you're starting up a business that requires a large initial investment. For example, assume you will need $100,000 over and above what you have available in your own cash or liquid assets to get the business going. Where and how are you going to raise this money? Will you be able to borrow from a friend? Are you going to take in a partner? Will you seek out a bank loan or a Small Business Administration loan, or will you seek out a private investor?

Regardless of where you will turn for outside financing, it is clear that

12

Money Key #5 will be most important in order for you to start your business.

If you are going to buy an existing business for about $100,000, you'll still have to find the start-up money from lenders, but you'll have an additional help. Many business owners are willing to accept as little as 20 percent down on the purchase and then allow you to pay them the rest on a monthly basis, out of profits.

BUYING A BUSINESS

Once you've decided what kind of a business you want to be in, the first question to ask is whether you start your own or buy an existing one. Many experts

Figure 2.2 Buying a Business

Advantages:	*Disadvantages:*
▪ Location is established	▪ The lease may be expiring
▪ Relationships with suppliers, sources all set up	▪ Redecoration or enlargement may be required
▪ Experienced employees are available	▪ Location may be poor
▪ Business records ready to help you plan	▪ Equipment may be outdated.
▪ Previous owner's experience is available while you are learning the business	▪ Inventory may be mediocre or old
▪ You know exactly how much it will cost to get into the business	▪ Current Employee problems
▪ Past profit picture and return on your investment can be more easily predicted	▪ Previous owner may have had unethical business practices that will affect the new business
▪ A favorable purchase price may be negotiated	▪ Potential competitors may present problems
▪ Shortens time it takes to establish the new business	▪ Poor financial records
▪ Customers are available immediately	▪ An unwise purchase due to desire to get started
▪ Initial financial outlay may be less than a new start-up	▪ Overall purchase price can be high
▪ Equipment, fixtures and leases are all set up	▪ Relationships with customers and suppliers may be unsatisfactory
▪ Supplies, inventory or materials are ready to go	

and owners believe that it's best to buy an existing business. The reasons are simple to see and there are many advantages and some disadvantages, as summarized in Figure 2.2.

With all these benefits, it's easy to understand why buying an established business is so often considered the best way to go. For first-time business owner with little or no experience, it can often seem to be a much safer way to ease into the business world. Equally important is the fact that the business buyer is established immediately. Most new, start-from-scratch ventures require a few years of intensive effort before profits start rolling in.

All the advantages of buying an existing business assume one thing: that the business you're buying is free of or has limited flaws. Just as when you buy a used car, it pays to be cautious. In almost every case, there will be problems to be overcome. One problem that frequently crops up is that the business seller doesn't want to accept a reasonable price because he or she confuses the value of the business (return on investment) with income (return on investment plus salary).

As with any purchase, the disadvantages of buying a business must be carefully thought about and considered, even if the deal goes through, as a means of getting the best purchase price.

Where To Find Businesses For Sale

The classified ads and business sections of local newspapers and The Wall Street Journal are full of business opportunities ads, offering businesses for sale. Likewise, you can advertise in these sections your interest in purchasing a business. You can place a classified ad in your local newspaper, usually under the listing title of "business opportunity wanted," or you can place a display ad in the business section of the paper. If you do not want to advertise your name or wish to keep people from knowing who you are, the newspaper will provide you with a return box number to which people can respond.

You may also get help from your lawyer or banker, who often will hear about people who for one reason or another want to sell their businesses. You may also want to send a letter to accountants, who often have clients that want to sell their businesses. Still other sources include business brokers, real estate agents and companies, business finders and firms, business opportunity shows and franchise shows.

If you really want to be bold and imaginative, then consider this: If you see a business that you like and would like to consider purchasing it, simply stop by or call the owner for an appointment. On meeting with the owner, state that you may be interested in purchasing his or her business. There is an old saying, "He or she who asks, gets."

Still another source for locating a business that may be for sale is to talk with the managers of the shopping centers of your area. They often are the first to hear when one of their tenants wishes to retire or sell their business.

A wide number of magazines that advertise different business opportunities for sale: Money, Entrepreneur, Income Opportunities, Success, and Business Start-Ups just to mention a few. These and many more can be found in your local library or at a nearby newsstand.

Buying the Company vs. Buying the Assets

Imagine the following plot: You have your eyes on Smith & Smith, Inc. It is a small, family-run business that manufactures rubber seals and gaskets. For the most part, the company consists of a workshop, including several machines, raw materials, an inventory of completed gaskets waiting for customers, some office furniture and equipment, and a delivery truck. Your initial negotiations indicate that Helen and Howard Smith are willing to sell for about $250,000.

The issue to be decided is whether you should purchase the corporation itself or only its assets. In the first case, you would purchase all the stock, the shares that are held by the Smiths; in the second case, you would buy only the material assets used by the company in its business.

As a general rule, you are better off buying just the assets because "you get what you see". This allows you to limit your liabilities or unknowns that you have received from the previous owner. From a financial point of view, you can claim immediate tax deductions for the inventory and other depreciable property.

Get a Lawyer

If you do find an existing business that seems like a good deal to take over, try to reach a verbal agreement with the owner on the major terms. Then see your lawyer right away. Besides offering legal protection, your lawyer will most likely help you in contract negotiations by obtaining useful supplementary information and data. He or she will give you valuable feedback before you leap into the water, before you put your signature on what might be the biggest deal of your life.

In addition to drafting the contract, your lawyer can review and evaluate documents prepared by the seller's lawyer and ask crucial questions that you might not even have thought of asking. Your lawyer can represent you at the closing procedures to ensure that all documents are handled correctly and to your advantage.

Your lawyer can also make you aware of what you need to know about the business. He or she can help you identify documents and records including existing leases for equipment, contracts for deed, pending lawsuits, federal requirements, and much more. Most important, an attorney can make sure that you don't sign before the other party has put all cards on the table.

15

Another important advantage an attorney can give you is positive or critical comments about the chances of the new business. When you don't have family members with relevant business experience, your attorney is the one who can listen patiently and can give objective advice when you spill out your hopes, fears and dreams for the future. Running a business can mean making good money; at the same time, it also means taking a risk. You need someone you can rely on; someone who will warn you before a potential risk turns into an actual disaster.

The Contract

Any contracts you make should be as detailed as possible. Don't be afraid of being a stickler. Have the seller list and briefly describe each item: equipment or parts thereof; vehicles; fixtures; furniture; inventory and raw materials, by number, weight or volume; work in progress; existing leases; rental agreements; patents; and real estate.

Make sure you have a written statement indicating who will be liable for the debts of the company at the time of the transaction. If it's you, make sure you know absolutely their full extent. In addition, there should be an agreement stating who is entitled to the accounts receivable. Be prudent and realistic. You may have trouble collecting some or all of the money outstanding, especially as a retailer in poorer neighborhoods.

After you have taken the preceding into consideration and have negotiated the purchase price, ask for an itemized statement, mainly for tax purposes. Here is an example:

Merchandise on hand	$ 80,000
Tangible personal property	$150,000
Lease agreements	$ 10,000
Good will/trade name	$ 10,000
Total purchase price	$ 250,000

If you have not already done so, this is the time to check with your financial source to determine how his or her people would feel about the deal and exactly how much they will be willing to provide to make it all work out.

Purchase Price Adjustments The idea of adjustments to the purchase price becomes especially important if there is a considerable time lag between the drawing of the contract and closing. So in setting out the purchase price, allow for adjustments. For example, make provisions for how to handle increases or decreases in merchandise on hand (inventory). One option might be to stipulate that you will pay up to $50,000 for inventory at closing, based on seller's invoice cost. If the actual inventory at closing exceeds this amount, you reserve the option of purchasing the difference, possibly at a discount.

Other adjustment provisions could include such items as pre-payments for rent or leases, utilities or insurance premiums, license fees and property taxes. Another important factor is salaries and wages. If they are paid at the end of each month retroactively and you take over the business at any other time, the purchase price should be reduced to allow for the fact that you are going to pay salaries for periods when the seller still owned the business.

Your purchase contract also should indicate when the payment for the company is due and how it will be executed (by check or promissory note, for example). Try to negotiate and be as creative as you can in your proposals. There are almost no restrictions or limits on the type of terms you can have if the seller consents.

Some transfers involve seller financing. Obviously, the number of installments and the applicable interest rate are key items for negotiations. In some instances, installments are tied to the profit generated during the first five years under new ownership. In those situations, the seller was willing or forced to continue to share in the risk of the business.

Most deals require a deposit when the contract is signed. Pay special attention at this point. Keep the deposit as small as you can and have in writing that it actually applies against the purchase price. Don't allow it to be treated as a form of fee. If you stretch your payments over an extended period of time, it's not unreasonable for the seller to retain a security interest in some of the major assets until payment has been made in full. Corresponding arrangements should be part of the general contract. In such a case, expect limited ownership or usage of major property items.

Think about these potential problems:

- The lease may be expiring and negotiations are needed.
- Redecoration or enlargement may be required.
- Location may be in a declining area.
- Equipment may require replacement or repair.
- Inventory may be unbalanced and/or outdated.
- Employees may be unionized, complicating contract terms.
- Relationships with customers and suppliers may have deteriorated.
- Profit potential may be endangered by stronger present or potential competitors.
- Financial records may not be a true reflection of value. This is a job for an accountant.
- Your desire to get started may cause an unwise purchase.
- Overall purchase price can be higher than the initial costs of a new start-up.

WHAT ABOUT FRANCHISING?

Figure 2.3 summarizes advantages and disadvantages of the small business option for franchising. The appeal of franchising for the independent businessperson is that it is a practical and economic means of fulfilling his or her desire for independence with a minimum of risk and investment and maximum opportunities for success through the use of a proven product or service and a proven marketing method. Franchising is a way to be in business for yourself, but not by yourself.

The franchisee is an independent business owner who pays the franchiser for the right to put this recipe for success to use. As a franchisee you provide all or nearly all the working capital to establish and develop the outlet. There is a continuous financial relationship, usually including a fee paid in advance, plus a continuing royalty based on an established percentage of gross revenues.

Some franchisers will supply financial assistance to the franchisee to pay the initial and ongoing costs of conducting the business. Although an attractive extra, financial assistance should not be considered as a major decision factor or a substitute for very careful, thorough investigation into all the facts in your choice of any franchise. It is simply another element that can be put into the mix.

Ideally, when you purchase a franchise, you are also purchasing a pre-packaged business. Although you own every part of it, you have a partner, your franchiser, who can insist or sometimes merely suggest how you run your business.

Why Do People Buy Franchises?

For the new entrepreneur, a franchise often makes it easier to go into business, because it cuts down on the amount of capital required and provides a sense of security through the experience and help offered by the franchiser. Franchising is one good way for some small business operators to avoid problems that can ruin a business.

The franchiser will usually help in such areas as site location, management training, financing, marketing, promotion, and record keeping. The franchisee, in return, agrees to operate under the conditions specified by the franchiser.

Figure 2.3 Buying a Franchise

Advantages:	*Disadvantages:*
<ul><li>Be in business for yourself, not by yourself</li><li>Maximum opportunities for success</li><li>Proven marketing methods</li><li>Minimum of risk and investment</li><li>Proven product or service</li><li>A pre-packaged business you own</li><li>Often reduces the amount of capital required</li><li>Security from experience and help the franchiser provides</li><li>A way to avoid problems that can ruin a business.</li><li>Help in such areas as site location, training, financing, marketing, promotion, and record keeping</li></ul>	<ul><li>Pay the franchiser for the right to use its program</li><li>Provide all or nearly all the working capital to establish and develop the business</li><li>A continuous financial relationship</li><li>Fee paid in advance</li><li>A continuing royalty based on a percentage of gross revenues.</li><li>The franchiser, can insist or suggest how you run your business.</li><li>Franchisee must agree to operate under specific conditions</li></ul>

THE BUSINESS CLIMATE

Whether yours is a start up, an established businesses or a franchise, it's always important to be aware of financial matters that can affect the profitability of your business.

Four key factors that can affect the performance of businesses are:

- Trends in the national economy
- Trends in your regional and local economies
- Trends in the industry or service in which you are involved
- The impact of new or proposed governmental (Federal, state and local) legislation and regulations on your business.

Although national economic indicators will show general trends, it's important to watch indicators that affect the local economic situation.

Understanding indicators such as local unemployment and inflation figures and interest rates will help you make financing and general business decisions. For example, higher interest rates could mean borrowing will be more expensive for small business, and lower interest rates may mean that you can borrow funds at lower cost. If unemployment figures are high and recession is likely, the local economy may not be receptive to the promotion of a new product or service or an additional location of an established business. Information about local indicators and forecasts can be found in local newspapers.

In addition to area indicators, it's important to understand local economic trends or developments. An expansion of services or introduction of a new product line by a large local employer could be a sign of the company's optimism toward future consumer spending. When major area employers are reducing their labor forces or when businesses seem to be closing their doors, the signal may be that the economy is slowing or stagnating.

Stay abreast of trends within your industry as well. For example, watch for new products that could be included in the present product line or any technological developments that may lower costs of production. Remember that trends and developments can benefit the competition as well, so keep in step by watching trends and technology carefully. Trade associations and industry newsletters can provide such information.

Federal and state legislation can influence your decision-making, directly and indirectly. For example, minimum wage legislation, importing or exporting regulations, or legislation that may prohibit the use of certain materials or chemicals are examples of federal legislation. Instances where state legislation affects small business are changes in sales tax or workers compensation, for example. The impact of legislation is often not felt immediately. This gives you time to adjust to new developments or regulations.

Pay close attention to economic indicators and information and use these tools in selecting and running your business. By tracking this type of information, your business expectations will be more realistic and planning objectives will be more practical.

CHAPTER 3

Success and The Five Money Keys

This chapter is about the role money plays in having a successful business. It describes the five Money Keys that have helped so many people like you reach business success. It will point out the importance of knowing the product or service you are selling, and that important ingredient, sales expertise, that makes it all work together.

We're going to talk about competition and the skills you already have or should develop before you even seek financing, because knowing yourself is the vital ingredient to getting others to give you money and making a go of whatever business you want to build and prosper.

In this chapter you will learn:

- The five Money Keys that will make your business a success.
- How you can learn valuable lessons from your competition.
- The capabilities it will take to make you successful a business operator.

No matter what skills or talents you bring to the business world, it is extremely unlikely that you will be a winner in this highly competitive world if you are not serious about money. Business is not a pastime or a hobby and should never be viewed as such. It is a serious enterprise in which only those who keep their eyes on the prize will eventually win out. The following five money keys are based on the experiences of a multitude of successful entrepreneurs. Read them carefully, it's some of the best advice you'll ever get.

THE FIVE MONEY KEYS

The five money keys that will make your business a success!

$ Money Key
Number 1 *The Successful Small Business Operator Has a Desire to Make Money!*

We've noted that the successful small businessperson must love to make money. But this is a different characteristic, this is the *desire* to make money. Four factors come into play when making this desire a reality: understanding the costs of doing business; making sure relationships with family and friends to not interfere with your business; and focusing your marketing efforts where it will help you the most.

The Costs of Doing Business

In order to make the money you desire, you must understand all the costs of doing business. For example, what are the total costs for a wholesale produce business? Include more than just the costs of the fruits and vegetables; include all of the other costs and expenses as well:

- Shipping both incoming and outgoing
- Warehousing
- Utilities for cold storage, telephone, heat, light and water
- Labor
- Selling expense
- Spoilage
- Packaging
- Insurance
- Bookkeeping
- Outside services such as legal and accounting
- Advertising
- and the list can go on and on.

Therefore, if you are in the wholesale produce business, you simply cannot look at only the cost of the produce you are purchasing for resale in order to set your selling price. Equally important, You must add something into the selling price for all of their other costs.

Relationship to Family and Friends

A second factor involved in the desire to make money is your relationship to family and friends. If you are to be successful in business, you have to treat the business as a business. For example, let us assume that, you have a clothing store. When a friend comes in to your store this does not automatically qualify her to make her purchase at cost or, at a substantial discount. You can't afford to treat family or friends any differently than any other customer. Don't "give away the store" just to be a nice guy. Yes, you may extend a courtesy discount. But, if every friend and relative was given extraordinary consideration, you are not going to be in business very long.

The same rule holds true for hiring new employees. Your personnel policy should be that you want to hire the most qualified individual at the most competitive salary. Jobs should not automatically go to relatives or friends Unless you feel that they are genuinely capable. Treat the business as a business when you extend courtesy discounts, when you hire employees and in one other area- advertising

Marketing

The purpose of marketing is to bring customers into your place of business, to give you the opportunity to make a sale. Marketing costs money. It is an expense and an investment. Therefore, you must be sure to treat your marketing efforts like any other purchase you make for your business.

If a church member comes to your place of business and says, "Will you please purchase an ad in our church program? After all, it is your duty as a member of the church! "You don't automatically say yes. Likewise, students from a local school may ask you to purchase an advertisement for their school sports programs. Again, simply because your place of business is close to the school, or your child may have attend the school, or you know one of the teachers, doesn't mean that you automatically place an advertisement in the sports program.

Ask yourself certain questions. Will the ad or marketing program bring in customers? What will the advertisement produce in the way of business for your firm? Who will the advertisement reach? Is the goodwill generated by my supporting the church or the school going to bring in more business? Are the church members, students, faculty or parents customers or potential customers for my business?

If your answers to these questions indicate that advertising in the high school sports program will do nothing or little for your business, then don't place an advertisement in it. However, if you do advertise in it and if you spend your advertising dollars in all of these "good will activities", don't look back later and wonder what happened to your advertising program? Don't say, "I spent all that money on advertising and got nothing out of it, so I am not going to advertise any more!" Using this kind of logic or coming to this conclusion is faulty and doing your business a terrible disservice.

On the other hand, if you want to make a contribution to the church or to the school, that's something else. Don't confuse your charitable contributions with legitimate business expenses. Advertising is an expense item for any business. Treat it like any other expense. Analyze it, study it, and be sure to purchase your advertising just like you would with any other item. That is, you want to receive the best buy for each dollar of expenditure or cost.

$ Money Key

Number 2 *The Successful Small Businessperson Knows All about the Features and Benefits of the Products or Services He or She Sells!*

In order to be successful, a small businessperson must be a complete expert on the product or service he or she is selling. For example, assume you are in the retail appliance business and you are selling television sets. A customer comes into your store looking for a 52" color TV set.

Why should the customer buy your product instead of someone else's. What are the features? Say, yours can show up to 10 channels on the screen at once. Or, it may have an automatic color system that maintains a perfect picture better than the competition's. And it may have built in super sound system. These features represent valuable benefits for the customer.

Being able to show multiple channels on the screen helps the user decide which to watch and helps assure that no attraction is being missed. The automatic color system adds value to this particular set. Finally, the super sound system adds to the enjoyment to the shows, especially films that have superior music and sound tracks.

Other dealers probably carry the same TV set, so your challenge is to give your customer a good reason to buy from you. That's called salesmanship. It's often been said that a good salesperson doesn't sell the steak, he or she sells the sizzle. But before you can sell that sizzle you have to be an expert on the products you are selling, the kind of services you can provide - and your costs of doing business. In the appliance business today, for example, the only profit a store makes can be in selling a long-term warranty at extra cost.

You may offer dollar savings to the customer, but you can't afford to sell products or services for less than your total cost of sales or without realizing a profit. It's one thing or the other, knowledge and salesmanship, lower prices or a reputation for superior service. You also have to know what your competition is doing and all the financial angles of buying, selling and stocking. In business, ignorance is not bliss, it can be fatal.

$ Money Key

Number 3 *The Successful Small Businessperson Knows How To Get Money From The Customer's Pocket Into His or Her Pocket!*

To accomplish this, you have to know your market. Who are your customers and prospects? Not necessarily by name and address. But how do you define them. Are they women, men, teenagers, senior citizens; or do they represent a cross section of all ages. How big is your market? How many customers and prospects are in your market? What is your trading area or, the geographic boundaries of your customer base?

If you are in the wholesale supply business, what types of businesses will purchase from you? All businesses? Metal manufacturers? Automobile dealerships? Just how are your customers defined.

Once the market is defined, the successful small businessperson must attract these customers and prospects to his or her place of business. What type of advertising appeals to your prospective customer? Which media or forms of advertising: television, newspapers, direct mail, radio, or billboards? What type of advertising themes: hard sell, soft sell, prestige advertising or price busting, repetitive advertising or sensational, ever-changing themes? How frequently do you advertise?

Know what appeals most to your customers and prospects. What are their "hot buttons"? What brings them to you rather then to a competitor? Above all, once your customer's attention, how do you get them to take money from their pocket and put it into yours?

$ Money Key

Number 4 *The Successful Small Businessperson Knows How Their Leading and Most Successful Competition Makes Their Money!*

A wise old sage once said, "We never invent the wheel, we simply reinvent it." That is very smart advice. Who says that we have to be totally creative in order to be successful? Why not look at the number one competitor in our area and either come as close to them as possible, copy them, or go one step better?

Look at McDonalds. They were early in the field of fast food and now they are the biggest and the best in their field. But were they the first? No. What about the old White Tower and White Castle Hamburger shops. A & W Root Beer, Toddle House, and the list could go on and on.

Ray Kroc, the founder of McDonalds simply copied them and went several steps further. Then look what happened. Wendy's, Burger King, Arby's, Jack in the Box and more came into the field with various levels of success. They simply copied one another, added a new twist here and there, and off and took off.

So if you want to be successful, look at your competition.

- Where are they located?
- How do they advertise?
- What services do they offer? Gift Wrap, delivery, charge accounts, repair services and so on.
- What hours are they open?
- What days of the week are they open?
- What product lines do they carry?
- If they are a service operation, what are their rates?
- What lines do they carry?
- What color, sizes, shapes do they offer?
- How big of an inventory do they have?
- How do they sell?
- Who are their key personnel?

To be a successful small business operator, you need to know almost as much about your competition as you do about yourself. This is not always easy. But it is simply amazing what you can find out about your competition if you set your mind to it. The important point being that if you can model your own business after a most successful competitor, your likelihood of success is greatly enhanced.

$ Money Key

Number 5 *The Successful Small Businessperson Knows How To Find and Use Someone Else's Money In Order To Make Money*!

Learning how to operate or start up your business on someone else's money is one of the most important lessons you'll learn in this book! It doesn't mean that you can go into or maintain a business without having to put in a single dollar. Yes, if you are going to start up a business, it's almost certain that you are going to have to use some of your own money. It may come from investments, savings, life insurance, a home equity loan or from the sale of some of your personal assets. But most likely, you do not have all of the necessary money to cover all the costs of starting a business. Or if the business is in full operation, there probably will come a time when you will need additional financing and will have to go out and get it.

Access to an unlimited source of operating funds is granted only to the federal government and a relative few, highly successful corporations. The rest of us do not have the luxury of having sufficient funds to start up a business or maintain one when times get tough.

A second luxury that most small businesspeople don't have is a business whose cash flow will generate immediate and continuing funds to start up or maintain business operations and growth. How wonderful it would be if we had a business that generated immediate cash to pay all of the start-up and operating expenses.

This means that we have to find a ready-made source of supply for your business's financial needs. The successful small business operator is acutely aware of this; usually the more successful a businessperson is, the more he or she knows about obtaining the necessary money for the business.

Money is available from a wide variety of sources: friends, relatives, loan companies, banks, customers, suppliers, the Small Business Administration, foundations, credit unions and insurance companies, among others.

Before exploring these many options, it's a good idea to examine yourself and your attitude toward money. That attitude must be positive with a capital *P*.

SKILLS INVENTORY

Following is a list of questions you might ask yourself to determine if you're right for a small business, or if a small business is right for you. By addressing your personal background, experience, aptitude, personal and business goals in this manner, you can realistically estimate your chances for success and can determine ways to sharpen your sharpen your approach to business matters. You'll better understand your abilities, weaknesses and the real person you are. You will identify your actual business goals, whether independence, money, business size, travel, people relations, status or something else. You'll get a better understanding of your personal goals, whether self-realization, creative expression, family, spirituality, physical health, or self-esteem.

Personal Attributes

1. Did you learn valuable lessons from businesses type activities in your childhood or teens?
2. Have you ever been fired from a job because of friction with or competition with your boss or upper management?
3. How would you rate yourself on these characteristics?

Desire to make money	__Good	__Average	__Poor
Hard Worker	__Good	__Average	__Poor
Special Talents	__Good	__Average	__Poor
Success oriented	__Good	__Average	__Poor
Sociable	__Good	__Average	__Poor

Organized	__Good	__Average	__Poor
Competitive	__Good	__Average	__Poor

4. Why do you want to go into business for yourself? Consider practical, measurable reasons and personal reasons.
5. In what ways do you expect your new business to change your life during the first year?
6. How persistent are you?
7. How interested are you in solving problems?
8. How good are you with details and keeping yourself organized?
9. Do you have success-oriented habits?

    Are you early to bed, early to rise?

    Do you keep yourself physically fit?

    Are your personal finances, always accurate or often behind and overdrawn?

    Are you careful about your personal appearance?

    Are you careful about keeping appointments, and promises?

    Are you always on time for meetings?
10. Do you generally like people or prefer to be alone?
11. Are you a steady worker or need a push from time to time?

Business Qualifications

1. What skills do you have that would help in your business?
2. What experience do you have that could be applied to your business?
3. Will your hobbies and interests be an asset to the business?
4. What abilities have you acquired from schools, seminars, and training?
5. Make a list of things you are confident you are good at. Think about your school, work, community, and home experiences. List things you have done well; for example, you might have organized a fund drive, finished a recreation room, or coached a Little League team.
6. Make another list of the skills you have developed over the years. Examples might include: I am a good salesperson; I can examine the facts and make sound decisions.
7. List your personal strengths. Examples might include: I am dependable; I am understanding.
8. List personal weaknesses you would like to improve. Examples might include: I am impatient; I am often late for appointments.
9. Prepare a list of the activities you do now or will do for your business. List the major items, such as producing the product or rendering the service, invoicing, paying bills, answering the phone, making sales calls and so on.

What all entrepreneurs have in common is that they're looking for the kind of independence and freedom that's possible only through business ownership. While this is a fine goal, it involves a wide range of problems you may never event think about when you are working for a salary.

Chapter **4**

What is Your Money Attitude?

You've thought long and hard about your business venture. You've done the research. You know exactly what you want to do and how you want to do it. You know what you're going to sell and how you're going to sell it. The next big step will be to get the money you'll need to turn those plans into reality. Before we go any further, however, it's important to take some time out to consider your attitudes about money and to understand some of the realities of borrowing.

Unless you have all the money you need, or a well-off and generous family, chances are you're going to have to use professional funding sources to get money to operate your business. Lenders and investors don't usually hand out money just because they like you or are impressed with the logic of your business idea. The golden rule in business is, he or she who has the gold makes the rules. If you go into the money market with unrealistic attitudes about money and the people who lend it, you're in for some disappointments and frustration.

This chapter will address some of the misunderstandings too many people have about money and borrowing. We'll also talk about the problems that face the loan providers you'll be contact, and how they operate.

WHAT IS MONEY?

If you think of money as something you use to buy goods or services, you're only partially correct. Money is also one way we keep track of our accomplishments. Consider the millionaires who continue to work day in and day out, long after they have all the money they'll ever need. They're typical of the way people often grade themselves and others by the bottom line on a financial statement.

It's important to understand your own attitude toward money before you make a loan request. Are you out to build a business, ensure financial success, or prove your ability to gain dollars just to be rich and influential? Your answer to this question can help or hinder the way you conduct your search for financing. The only practical way to obtain financing is to view the loan process objectively. This is a business arrangement, pure and simple.

COMMAN MISCONCEPTIONS

If you think of lenders as narrow-minded bureaucrats whose only interest is digging into your personal life and whose only pleasure results from defeating your dreams, think again. For example, do you share any of these mistaken beliefs?

- Being in debt is bad business.
- A good personal credit rating should make business borrowing easy.
- Financial information should be kept secret.
- Business debts should have nothing to do with personal funds.
- Lenders should appreciate that business is unpredictable.
- Bankers get too involved in other people's business.
- Lenders have no imagination; they can't recognize a good idea.
- Nobody tells lenders the truth
- Banks lend money only to people who don't need it.

Anyone who has ever applied for a loan might find these and the following attitudes a little strange. Bankers have heard them all. We will consider these feelings and see how they can keep you from getting a loan.

Being in Debt Is Bad Business

It's a good rule to be careful with money, but there are times when it will be necessary to borrow funds. Think of money as a tool that helps your business reach its goals. Not borrowing money when it is needed, and can be safely paid back, is as foolish as borrowing too much money that can't be repaid.

A Good Personal Credit Rating Should Make
Business Borrowing Easy

You'd like to believe that your personal record for repaying loans should be enough to qualify you for a business loan. You know that you'll always pay back a loan; you always have.

A business loan is different. It is generally for a larger amount than any individual could easily repay. A business loan has to be paid back by the business. If your company can't produce enough to pay the loan, the bank will not get its money, even if the people who own the business honestly intend to pay their bills. That's why you will have to show the lender how the business is going to repay its loan. It's important to realize that in order to break even, a bank must make 97 good loans to make up for one bad loan.

Financial Information Should Be Kept Secret

When you borrow money the lender in a sense your business partner. The lender needs to understand your financial status. Any lending institution needs to know what you are doing with your money to evaluate the likelihood of its being repaid. Your banker can be trusted with your personal and business financial information. If you ever doubt this, get a new banker, but never withhold information that the banker needs to properly analyze your loan request.

The owners of older, more established businesses may feel the company has proven itself and does not need such invasions of privacy. Don't let this become a part of your thinking. A banker can't do the best job for you and your company if he or she doesn't have all the needed financial tools.

Business Debts Should Have Nothing To Do With Personal Funds

One test lenders use is to see if you believe in your company enough to risk all or part of your personal assets. They could decide that if you don't have enough confidence to guarantee the debt, you should not be borrowing the money. Some large and well-fixed companies can borrow money without personal guarantees but smaller organizations often have to pass this test of confidence.

Lenders Should Appreciate That Business Is Unpredictable

No one has the foresight to accurately predict the future, but that doesn't mean you can't make a businesslike forecast about how your company will develop. If you don't at least make a try, you can't expect a lender to get an idea of how you will pay the loan back. It's your responsibility to put together appropriate plans and share them with your banker. Even if your first plan doesn't pan out, with

31

experience, you'll soon get better at forecasting.

Bankers Get Too Involved In Other People's Business

Some people are afraid their lender will take control of their company's success or failure. A good banker can often make a difference in how a company develops, but contribute fully if you're not willing to share information. You have half the responsibility of creating an open and clear connection. At the same time, you are always free to accept suggestions or reject them. Bankers are in the business of making good loans and they are always out to make the best loan record they can.

Lenders Can't Recognize A Good Idea

You'll never know unless you ask. If you don't have confidence in your company and your loan request, it will be difficult for the lender to have confidence in you. If you have a good business idea, act with confidence, explain your case and ask for the loan. Don't risk leaving the lender in the dark as to whether you really wanted financing or were just fishing for information.

Nobody Tells Lenders The Truth

Getting financing is important, but establishing an ongoing business relationship is just as important. You never know when you'll have to go back to the well for more money. Being truthful with the lender, repaying your loans and fulfilling all your commitments will help to establish your business credit rating not only with your initial lender but for any financial dealings you'll have in the years to come. Trust creates the basic setting in which all business is conducted. Lenders and suppliers need to know that you are a dependable person with whom they will want to do business.

Banks Lend Money Only To People Who Don't Need It

This misconception is based on the fact that financial institutions want to be sure that borrowers have the means to repay their loans. They cannot afford to hand out money without a reasonable expectation that they'll get their money back and make a profit on the transaction.

Your responsibility is to convince the lender that your business is one that can and will pay back its loan. On any day in the United States, hundreds of billions of dollars remain outstanding in business loans. People who don't need money don't take out loans, so obviously plenty of businesses that need financial help and are getting it.

WHAT THE LENDER THINKS

Lending institutions are in the business of making loans, which they expect to be paid back and be profitable for them. They want to make loans and they really do try to accommodate their customers. At the same time, they have to be careful about whom they lend money to and how they do it. Compare lending to a business that sells a product and consider how company owners would feel about not getting paid for the products they sell.

Lenders want to lend you money if they can see their way clear to doing it safely. Unfortunately, this is not always the case. There are other concerns that affect a banker's judgment.

A Loan Proposal Must Be Convincing

If the banker grants a loan, a lengthy process begins in which his or her reputation, judgment, and, perhaps job, will be put on the line.

The lender must review the loan request carefully, prepare a write-up for a loan committee or loan supervisor, and support the loan request under close questioning from bosses and associates.

Next, he or she must prepare the loan documentation and the necessary reports. The loan officer has to follow up after the loan is made and take action if collection might be necessary. The loan officer has to explain and defend the loan if any problems develop.

You can see why it is easier, and often safer, for a loan officer to simply turn down a loan. On the other hand, a loan officer who doesn't make loans will not have a job for long. A good loan proposal must convince lenders that it is in their interest to lend money to you.

A Loan Rejection Is Not A Personal Insult

Attitudes toward borrowing and lending affect a company's success in obtaining proper financing. Your challenge is to recognize and overcome your negative attitudes and misconceptions about money and borrowing. Then, with a good loan proposal, you can overcome any negative feelings the lender might have.

When a lender refuses to make a particular loan, the reason usually is that there are sound reasons to believe the loan will be a poor risk. A loan refusal is only one lender's estimate of the uncertainty involved in that loan request. It is not a judgment of your worth as a person.

Don't let your fear of rejection stand in the way of getting proper financing. If you make a habit of taking a loan refusal as a personal insult you can get into a mind-set that will make it difficult to obtain a loan anywhere. If you approach a lender with a resentful attitude, the lender may think that you don't have the open-minded attitude needed to run a business. That's strike one against you.

You get a second strike if you approach a potential lender with the attitude that you will probably be turned down because you were refused by a lender before. Be positive: Every loan application is a new beginning. Every newly approached lender gives you a fresh opportunity to make your case better. Learn the lessons or your previous rejections and do not to repeat them.

One mistake some inexperienced people make is to try to feel out a lender without actually asking for the loan. If you hide your needs behind statements such as: "I don't really need the money, but would you lend it to me if I asked?" or "What is your bank's attitude toward first-time business loans?" you're fooling no one but yourself. Playing games with bankers, who really are practical businesspeople, is poison to the process.

Chapter 5

Business Planning

There are many reasons for preparing a business plan; each in itself is sufficient for getting the job done before you proceed any farther in the process of starting or expanding your business. Regardless of the specific reason, however, the underlying goal of preparing a business plan is to ensure the success of the business.

The main reasons for preparing a business plan are as follows:

- A business plan will help you think through the type of business you are starting and will raise the questions you need to answer to succeed in your business. Careful consideration of your plan will also tell you whether you should NOT proceed in developing the business.
- A well-crafted business plan will help you obtain financing. Whether your are staring up a small business or maintaining an existing one, banks and financial institutions want to see that you know where you are, where you want to go and how you plan to get there.
- It helps you map the course of your business, thus allowing you to make detours, change direction and set your own pace for starting and running the business.
- Through planning, you can establish a system of checks and balances for your business so that you avoid mistakes.
- By setting goals and standards in your plan, and comparing these with

35

industry standards, you can set up benchmarks to assess progress.

- Careful planning requires that you assess your business's strengths, as well as those of your competition. This will help you develop the competitive spirit to make your business a success.
- The planning process forces you to think through the entire business process; by doing this, you will be likely to start your business prepared and armed with information vital to opening and maintaining your business.

PREPARING YOUR PLAN

In short, the two main reasons why a business plan is prepared are to (1) help you run your business, and (2) determine how you are going to finance it.

A business plan addresses many different elements and areas of business operations. Figure 5.1 is a suggested outline for your business plan. Read through it and check off areas that do not apply to your business; then check the ones for which you already have information. Now you can concentrate on those for which you will have to prepare material.

THREE KINDS OF PLANS

Now that you know what planning is, you can decide how much you'll have to do in order to make the most of your efforts. Try to think of your business as a series of different plans that work together; only the very simplest businesses can do everything with one plan.

Plans can cover different time periods. There are three basic planning models: long-term, mid-term and short-term plans. These plans address the following elements of running a business:

- *Financing.* How much money will you need? Where are you going to get it? When will you need it?
- *Marketing.* How will you sell your product or service? Who will do it?
- *Distribution.* How will you get your product or service to your customers? What limitations do you have to take into consideration?
- *Production.* How will you do or make what you sell? Who will be responsible for keeping it on track?

Beyond these projections you may need various plans to keep you business running smoothly. Planning will help you work things out on paper first, and enable you to set up procedures or systems to handle those things that are routine for your business. Not all parts of a business plan are looked at equally. If you are presenting your plan to a potential funding source, you need to concentrate on the financial projections part of the plan and how those numbers will be achieved.

Figure 5.1 Business Plan Items

Description of Business	Don't Need	Have Material	Have to Prepare
Title Page			
Table of Contents			
Executive Summary			
Industry, Market and Competition			
Industry Definition			
Market Definition			
Products and Services			
Initial Products and Services			
Proprietary Features			
Future Products and Services			
Marketing Plan			
Marketing Overview			
Marketing Objectives			
Strategy – Advertising, Promotion, and Public Relations			
Sales Methods			
Production Plan			
Facility Requirements			
Equipment Requirements			
Labor			
Production Process & Capacity			
Technology Needs			
Management Team			
Management Team			
Business Advisors			
Personnel Needs			
Financial Plan			
Summary			
Projected Income Statements			
Projected Balance Sheets			
Cash Flow Projections			
Sources and Uses of Funds			
Appendices			
Biographies of the Principals			
Personal Financial Statements			

Long-Term Plans

Long-term plans include your financing plan and your strategic plan which are essentially the blueprints of how you want your business to operate and develop.

A combined financing and strategic plan is a business plan, and should cover your expectations for the next three to five years.

Your banker or financing source usually will require one or both of these plans. The reason for this is simple: They expect to make a long-term commitment to you, and they won't feel comfortable doing that unless they can see into your crystal ball and understand your best estimate of what is going to happen down the road. You'll probably do only one or two of these, and you should check them every six months or so to assess your progress.

Mid-Term Plans

A mid-term plan will include your big objectives, such as launching new products, opening up new sales territories or building a strong staff.

After doing some research, entrepreneurs can usually handle the kind of estimating required for planning at this level. Mid-term plans cover one to three years, and should be reviewed about every month.

Short-Term Plans

These are the operational, day-to-day plans that cover the procedures that get the work out, the orders filled, and the deliveries made on time. Resourceful entrepreneurs usually have no trouble in this area; however, it is easy to get caught up or distracted by these short-term concerns.

Because short-term planning can be so interesting and challenging, it can sometimes take attention away from long-range problems. In other words, it's fine to stick to your knitting, but don't forget that you have to buy yarn in advance. In the same way, it's important to plan your product line to match your selling seasons. Short-term plans should be reviewed daily or weekly, depending upon your production schedule.

Preparing a business plan is important in itself. At the same time, much of the information you will have collected for it will be used to create the loan proposal that will be the heart of your application to lenders.

The really smart people, who do a lot of planning, say that about 85% of what's going to happen in your business can be anticipated; therefore, you can have a plan in place to deal with most situations. The remaining 15% are the crises, the things you absolutely have to address when they come up. With proper planning your business runs itself instead of running you, so you will have the time and patience you'll need to give proper attention to all the unforeseen problems that will pop up in even the best run business.

Chapter 6

Know Your Market and Your Competition

Nothing is more important in planning for business success than knowing your market and your competition. You may have a great product or a truly exceptional service, but the dollars won't roll in if your competitors do a better job of getting those customers than you do. Equally important, your financial plan will miss an important element, which will certainly be obvious to any lender.

WHAT IS YOUR MARKET?

Nothing sells itself and no one can sell to the wrong market, not even the mythical salesman who can sell freezers to Eskimos. In this chapter, we're going to talk about some of the factors that will help you identify your market and win over enough customers to move dollars from their wallets to yours. You will also learn how to think about your business from the point of view of your potential customers.

Discover Your Real Business

The makers of horse-drawn carriage makers went out of business early in this century, because they forgot what their real business was. It wasn't making carriages, although that's what they sold. Their real business was transportation,

39

moving people from one place to another. Because they forgot what was important to their customers, their customers moved on without them. Automobiles, streetcars and trains gave them what they needed more conveniently and at a better price. Before you could say, "going out of business sale," the market for horse-drawn carriages disappeared. Had they realized what their customers really wanted, they could have gotten a head start on the next business opportunity or found something else to sell.

The strength of any business is in its ability to meet the changing needs of its customers. And changing customer creates new opportunities for customer-focused and future-oriented entrepreneurs.

To get a genuine fix on what it takes to get and keep customers you have to answer to such questions as the following:

- What are you really selling?
- Who are your customers?
- Where will they come from?
- What types of products and/or services do your customers want?
- Should you sell name-brand or off-brand products?
- What types of products and/or services do they not want?
- What type of advertising and promotion will attract customers?
- Will you be selling wholesale, retail, Internet or a combination?

Identifying the market for your products or services is a critical to business success. Unfortunately, a small business simply cannot afford to make a large investment in something that might not work. Of course, success can never be guaranteed but there are ways to reduce some of the risks you'll have to take.

As you plan to make good on your ideas, keep your customers and potential customers foremost in mind. Think about what is really important to your customers, and you will have the vital key to your business operations.

The first question to ask is: Why will customers buy from you?

- Is it the kind of product or service you offer?
- Is the product or service unique?
- Is it the quality of product or service you offer?
- Is it because you can fill their orders faster and ship the same day?
- Is it because you deliver?
- Is it for convenience; are you close to their homes or on a major business street?
- Is it because your business is located in a busy mall?
- Is it because customers can walk in on their lunch hour?
- Are your customers so loyal that they will drive 10 miles out of their way to buy from you?

Then ask yourself how you will operate my business to keep it a going concern?

- Is it better to buy or rent a location?
- How will rent or lease costs affect prices?
- Will you need employees with specialized talent or training?
- Will you have to beat your competition's prices?
- Do you need an inexpensive labor pool to keep my costs low?
- Should you locate near a bus line?
- Do you need a parking lot next to my premises?
- Do you need to be close to the airport for quick shipments?
- Would a shopping center be the best location?
- Do I need any specialized technology to compete?

MARKET RESEARCH

All your planning should be based on the answers to questions such as the preceding. You may already know some of the answers, but you should be prepared to do careful research to get at what your customers really think. Market research may confirm some ideas you already have; just as likely, you may get some surprises. Either way, you'll have some valuable information that can help you make more intelligent decisions.

If you're lucky, you will uncover unmet customer needs. It's a genuine thrill for an entrepreneur to learn something new about his or her market can provide a competitive edge. Think what you would be able to do if you could discover a need in the marketplace that had not yet been filled. Armed with this information, you could be the only one with the missing product or service, which means you could have all of the market share to yourself.

The process of marketing research involves analyzing your competition, suppliers, and new customers. You don't have to spend a lot of money on a marketing expert; there's a free source of help at the Small Business Development Center or the SCORE office in your area, who can provide you with free advice on how to develop an effective marketing program.

To find the offices nearest you, simply look them up on the Internet at www.sba.gov or call the Small Business Answer Desk at 800-827-5722.

Asking The Right Questions

Market research can be done by anyone who is able to ask questions, record the information, and learn what it means. It can be done by you or someone you hire. There are questions you can ask to accomplish this, depending on your situation.

Starting a Business If you are about to start-up a business, you might want to know the following:

- Who are your potential customers?
- How different is your product or service from what is on the market now?
- Would your product or service be more attractive at a lower price than competition's?
- Would your product or service be more attractive at a higher price than competition's? (Some products respond well to a higher selling price that implies higher quality)
- What are the long-term trends that will affect your business?
- How will location impact your business?
- Who are your competitors?
- What products and/or services do they offer?
- What is their sales volume?
- Where are they located?

Building an Existing Business If yours is an established business, your market research will have a slightly different slant. You can use the information you already have before you look anywhere else. There is a wealth of details at your fingertips, in your own records, that is not available to the person who is not yet in business:

Where does your patronage come from? Start with asking existing customers exactly why they buy from you. Customer addresses, on sales receipts or credit applications, will give a sense of your primary market area. Customer phone numbers will provide you with the same kind of information - just check with the phone company to find out the areas of your community to which the prefixes (the first three digits) are assigned.

Take a local map and mark an X everywhere you have a customer; then look at where they are concentrated. Is there a pattern? If there is, you may be able to concentrate your advertising dollars more effectively.

Then there are some questions you can answer from your own day-to-day experiences and a little searching in the records:

- Is your advertising reaching the people you think are your best customers?
- Have your customers' spending habits changed?
- Have your competitors made any recent changes?
- What services should you offer customers?
- Should you offer some items you don't offer now?
- What hours should your business be open?
- What important changes have taken place in the market?

Of course, you can easily alter or add to the list to meet your individual needs.

Once you clearly determine the direction you want your business to take and what is most important to your customers, you are ready to begin exploring your market in detail. In the research process you will be able to attach definite numbers to your plans and confirm or change your operating direction.

FINDING THE RIGHT CUSTOMERS

For start-up or existing businesses, a key element to success is finding the right people to target as your customers. The time you invest at the front end will pay big rewards for years to come.

Who are the right people? They are the ones most like those with whom you'll be doing business, who will have an interest in or a need for what you have sell. At this point, you will have to do some "blue-sky" thinking. Make a list of everything you now know about the kinds of people who you can expect to buy from you. This could include factors such as:

Income level	Location	Age
Sex	Buying habits	Special interests
Education	Home ownership	Age of home
Race	Skills	Food habits
Religion	Hobbies	Marital Status
Health	Household pets	Vacation styles
Job description	Number of children	Age and type of cars
Physical handicaps	Do-it-yourself types	Spare time activities

Plus many others as they apply.

If you plan a business-to-business company, develop a similar list from a business standpoint.

When all the factors which apply to your potential customers are described completely, you have what is called a customer profile. It could be a detailed outline, as it would be if you were selling chair lifts to handicapped homeowners. Or, it could be a broad profile, as it would be if you were opening a photography studio like in Figure 6.1.

Where to Find Customers

Once you identify your potential customers, how do you find them? You can begin your research at your local library. By using regional maps and reference materials, you can save a lot of time and discover what trends will affect potential sites. The reference materials you will need are found in:

- Current data from the latest census (www.census.gov)
- City or town hall population and business surveys
- Local statistical information
- Chamber of Commerce
- Business organizations
- Local newspapers

Figure 6.1   Customer Profile for the Real Clear Photo Studio

Customers	Characteristics	Where to Find Customers
Wedding Parties	Average age 20-35 Bride and groom are normally decision makers	Churches Bridal Shops Newspaper announcements Graduation lists
Baby or Family Portraits	Families	Birth announcements Single family home owners Baptism announcements
Commercial Photo Work	Business establishments Advertising agencies	Chamber of Commerce Yellow Pages Business Directories

Your librarian will be happy to assist you in finding the best information for your community.

Other sources that can help you tap into helpful marketing information:

State governments Most state governments have business census information and economic data on the various industries and business activities for their own states. In addition, specific departments within each state have data. For example:

- Many state Divisions of Motor Vehicles sells information from driver's licenses and motor vehicle registrations. With this, for example you can identify all the owners of Cadillacs or owners of imported automobiles.
- State licensing and regulatory offices can supply you with listings of doctors, lawyers, real estate agents, and even delicatessen owners.

44

- Your state Census Data Center can identify those zip codes in which you can more likely find young parents who can afford designer clothes for their children. The state government operator in your state capitol can help you locate the specific office that may be able to help you.
- Your state highway department can provide information on traffic flows; that is, how many vehicles drive in a particular direction at all time on a give highway.

Federal Government Finding many of the marketing facts you'll need for proper planning doesn't have to be expensive. The federal government employs thousands of experts whose job it is to gather information which entrepreneurs can use, on all kinds of businesses:

- The U.S. Dept. of Agriculture can give you information on the market for thousands of products, including house plants, diets, aquaculture, and even bull sperm.
- The U.S. Department of Commerce can give you the latest information on hundreds of products, including golf balls, computers, toys, or biotechnology.
- The U.S. International Trade Administration provides marketing information on items as video games, mushrooms, and broom handles.

The U.S. Government's Federal Information Center can help you locate a nearby office that can help you.

The Government as a Customer Federal and state governments buy all kinds of products and services. They are always in the market for all kinds of products and services, including freelance writers, artists, computer consultants, even janitors. Every U.S. Representative's office has access to a computer database that keeps track of all the current government contract opportunities for businesses. By contacting your representative, you can have him or her do a computer search to find out if the government is looking for products or services that your business provides. This same function is now available over the Internet. The same is true for the Small Business Development Centers and Procurement Assistance Offices in your state.

Local Sources The following entities can provide good information about your community:
- Look to your local banks. They are in the business of providing service to businesses and individuals, so they usually keep reliable, up-to-date information on population and business trends for their areas.
- Chambers of Commerce or local business organizations know which

businesses are in town. They also know about new businesses which are planning to move into an area or established ones that are moving out. They probably can help you estimate how much business you may expect to do, particularly if there is, or was, a similar business in the area.

- Another source of good information is your area newspaper. The local paper makes it its business to know about your city. Talk to an editor about changes in the community. Advertising sales managers are often the best source of information since they are out on the street everyday.

KEEPING CUSTOMERS

Finding customers is only half the story of a successful business; you also need to know how to keep them. To do that, you need to know how to develop good customer relations through honest and effective advertising, warranties, product safety, and complaint handling procedures. For free copies of Consumer Affairs Guides For Business: Contact the Office of Consumer Affairs, U.S. Department of Commerce, Washington, DC 20230 or call 202-377-5001.

FINDING THE RIGHT LOCATION

If you are seeking information for site location, keep in mind the following two key concepts:

First, most retail businesses draw most of their customers from a predictable trade area around their location. You must depend on the people within this trade area to provide the majority of your customer base. Each type of business has a different size trade territory. By projecting the size of the trade area your type of business can expect, you can draw a circle on a map of the city around each site you are considering to help select the best location.

The "convenience factor" that determines the size of your primary trade area. Popular businesses, such as food stores, neighborhood restaurants and gas stations, draw most of their business from trade areas as small as one-half mile in diameter. Shopping centers can draw from a 35-mile radius. Trade areas don't have to be just geographical circles, however. You will attract customers from many miles away if your location is on a major thoroughfare, visible from a freeway, or close to a large office complex or university. You must be satisfied that you have made it as easy as possible for your customers to buy from you by locating near them in a place that is easy to find.

Second, think like your prospective customer. Forget your personal preferences. You have to please your customers, now and in the future, to make the most of your venture.

Your research into population information will help you answer questions like these about your potential customers:

- How many persons or families are in the trading area and how has this changed over time?
- Is the area growing in population or declining?
- Where do your potential customers work? What do they do for a living?
- How much money does the average household earn per year?
- How many young people live in the area?
- How many old people live in the area?
- How many families live in the area?
- How many have young people or small children?
- How many one-person households are there?
- How many single-family homes are there? Apartments? Condominiums?
- How many rent?
- What is the average monthly rent?
- How many families own homes? What is the value of the homes?
- How many of the families own one automobile? How many own two?
- How many other businesses are located in the trading area?
- What types of businesses are they?
- Will they attract potential customers to you?

Now that we've covered the many angles of determining your best market, we're ready to show you methods that will help you analyze competition to help you anticipate problems and prepare to meet many of the problems that all businesses face.

KNOW YOUR COMPETITION

Whether your business idea involves a product, a service or a retail establishment, you can't ignore your competition. Even the newest, most unique business concepts have competition. Retailers or manufacturers of similar products are obvious competitors, but consider also such situations as movie theaters and video stores; any time a customer rents a videotape, that's one less time he or she will go out for an evening, and one less opportunity for the theater owner to profit not only from ticket sales but concession sales of popcorn, soda and so on.

Your competitors are after the same thing you are: profits. To ensure your piece of the pie, you have to know who your competitors are and how your offering stacks up against theirs. A careful examination of the competition will not only prepare you for intelligent business planning, it will also be an important part of the package you will have to show lenders when you go out for financing. For many lenders, a business plan without details on the competition raises a red flag, making them doubt its quality and thoroughness. They also react negatively to plans that put down the competition.

There are three types of competitors: Direct, Indirect and Future.

Direct Competitors

Direct competitors are those who seek the same customer base you are targeting, with the same product or service. When judging direct competitors, it's not enough to compare their basic offerings with yours. The more complex your business is, the more you need to look at each element that goes into why and how the competitor is succeeding or failing.

Indirect Competitors

Indirect competition involves products or services that are going after the same dollars from the same customers you're after. If you want to open a computer store, the mass marketer in the next town is your indirect competitor. If you plan to start-up a delicatessen, you must consider the impact of the fast-food outlet down the block that is competing for the same dollars. Indirect competition can be a major factor in retail and customer-oriented services.

A florist might consider other florists as direct competition but ignore the local supermarket that has a plant department. If the supermarket has better parking, friendlier service, quality products, and good prices, it can substantially cut into the florist's business.

Future Competitors

How can the forecast future competitors? The key is anticipation. Competitive situations change rapidly with each new development in marketing and technology. Staying current with the business picture and anticipating market trends, what people will want tomorrow, will not only put you ahead of the game but is sure to impress lenders and investors.

KNOW HOW YOUR COMPETITORS MAKE MONEY

Success in business takes more than simply knowing who your competitors are. It's vital to know how your competitors make money.

You have to be familiar with their product or service line pricing, hours of business, and a whole list of other items. You have to understand their marketing strategies: how they sell, how they merchandise and advertise. Knowing these things is a big step toward success in business. Better still is to get to know how the number one competitor in the field does it and then go it one step further to be a better marketer.

The automobile companies are outstanding examples of this. They copy one another's styling, warranty programs and rebate offers. Department stores and grocery store chains take leads from each other in using successful advertising campaigns such as loss leaders, couponing and special services.

For companies involved in manufacturing, it is vitally important to be fully aware of leading competitors' design and performance features and the benefits they deliver. And, as in any other business, they must be constantly attuned to new developments.

Obviously, competition varies from business type to business type. It is important to consider each competitor individually and work up an information sheet for each one, including answers to the following questions:

- How profitable is the business?
- What is its sales volume?
- What is their return on investment?
- Where it is located?
- How many and what types of employees it has?
- What is its average sales per employee?
- How it is set up as a business (e.g., sole proprietorship, partnership, corporation)?

Add any other information that you think might help you understand how these businesses work. If you can. also include the following industry figures:

- Total Sales
- Cost of goods sold
- Gross profits
- Selling expenses
- Leasehold expenses
- Inventory expenses
- Office and computer expenses
- Administrative expenses
- Tax expenses (payroll, property, and taxes other than federal
- Miscellaneous expenses
- Net profits before income taxes

For major competitors, consider any appropriate information on how they do business and how successful they have been. Add in any findings of any market research you have done. If your business is different from the competition in any significant way, whether financially or in distribution methods, how do you account for this difference? If you can find out, consider what the competition thinks of your business concept?

Recognize any other indirect sources of competition you see in the marketplace (remember the video store and the movie theater). Get sales figures, growth rates, and as much of the information mentioned above as you can for each of these.

You'll want to make a survey of what competitors charge for the type of product or service you are proposing. List how your prices will compare with competitors prices.

SOURCES OF COMPETITIVE INFORMATION

There are many sources of competitive information; most of it shouldn't cost you a cent more than providing a cup of coffee or traveling to see the people who know what you need to know.

Wholesalers and Manufacturers

These businesses are good sources of information about a particular market, its customers and competition. Wholesalers, manufacturers and retailers generally know the trends in their business and will be pleased to help you. After all, when you go into business, they expect you'll be buying from them!

Federal and State Governments

The U.S. Department of Commerce field service offices throughout the country can provide you with relevant information. The government also publishes reports on specific markets, industries and products, which may be of use to you. Likewise, you can obtain information from various state departments of commerce or business.

Trade Associations

The trade associations which serve a particular industry are excellent sources of information about your industry and market. Your local library may have a directory of trade associations.

Business Publications

Every industry has magazines, newsletters or pamphlets written exclusively for and about itself. These can either be local or national. Many trade association produce these publications. For more information, contact the sources listed under

"Trade Associations," above.

Media Representatives

The advertising salespersons who represent magazines, newspapers, radio and television stations are usually a fine source of market information. Many of their companies maintain extensive research departments for this express purpose, and the information they have is free.

Competitors

It is amazing what you can learn by going directly to your competitors and asking for information, advice and help. If you feel uncomfortable about going to your direct competition, try contacting a business owner located in the next city or the next state. Keep in mind, however, that information from a competitor, located even a short distance from you, may not necessarily apply to your business. If you can ask the right people the right questions, then interpret and apply the information to your best advantage, you'll be in an excellent position to plan intelligently.

The worksheet plan in Figure 6.2 will help you assemble the type of information discussed in this chapter. You can use the worksheet as is or adapt it to your particular purposes. Once you have organized the information on your product, your market and your competition, it's time to dive into the subject of how to go about getting the financing to get your business going and growing. That's what we'll discuss in the next chapter.

UNDERSTANDING THE COMPETITION WORKSHEET

DIRECT COMPETITION

The businesses that provide similar products in our area are:

The best marketers of similar products:

Primary competitors' estimated market share is:

Best prospects for winning away market share include:

Our location relative to competition (advantages and disadvantages) include:

Consumer awareness of key competitors indicates:

Our main competitive edge is

Attach a summary of competitive pricing, warranty policy, promotional incentives, distribution network, and other factors.

INDIRECT COMPETITION
Our indirect competition comes from

We expect this to grow/decline for the following reasons:

We expect the following competitive trend:

With the information you will have assembled on your product, your market and your competition, it's time to dive into the subject of how to go about getting the financing to get your business going and growing.

Chapter 7

Estimating Money Needs

Every start-up business or established company must determine its real financial needs. At first glance, it would seem that no company can have too much money; but even a good company can fail if it's short of funds. A business can also run into trouble if it has too much financing and has difficulty paying back loans.

What's most important is to determine the level of funding that will ensure proper operations without placing a strain on debt repayment. Before you can sensibly estimate how much money you will need, however, you have to know exactly what you plan to do. Think of any sort of business planning activity as an opportunity to ensure your business's success. Only by thinking through your business logically and systematically, from initial idea to final product or service, will you be able to realistically determine financial needs.

CASH FLOW MANAGEMENT

To a small business, cash flow management is more than simply matching dollars in with dollars out. In fact, the way you manage cash can have a major impact on your profitability. One simple way to begin an analysis of your cash flow needs is to divide funds into three categories, each of which can be managed to enhance your bottom line:

1. Incoming funds
2. Outgoing funds
3. Static funds

Incoming Funds

These are the revenues that come into your business from sales made to customers either for cash or credit. Cash flow is the lifeblood of any business, so it's crucial to keep that money flowing in, to maintain control of your cash receivables. Your profits can suffer when you have money tied up in past-due receivables.

A favorable cash flow statement can be a big help when you need to go to the bank to borrow funds.

Outgoing funds

These are the operating expenses that flow out of the business. They include accounts payable, salaries, taxes, and other items necessary to conduct your business. If current cash expenses are too high and putting a drain on cash, banks and others might look negatively on such a situation.

Static funds

These include the cash and inventory that you keep on hand. They add nothing to your bottom line. These can also include:

- Raw materials
- Consumables
- Fixed plant and equipment (buildings, forklift trucks, machinery, etc.)
- Office machines
- Office furniture
- Trucks and other vehicles

Static funds can be used to enhance your cash position. For example you can deposit your available cash in a safe interest-bearing account as funds come in, so there's no reason to let your cash sit idly.

BUDGETING

The core of your business planning is the cash budget, which translates operating plans into dollars. Without a cash budget, you have no way of estimating financial needs. Few investors or creditors will even consider a request for money without one.

The cash budget helps a lender answer these important questions:
- How much money do you need?
- How will you spend the money?
- How soon will you pay us back?

The entrepreneur who is put off by numbers misses their important role in the efficient operation of any business venture. An understanding of financial matters is as important to a venture's survival and growth as production, marketing and other basic business functions.

Because most small businesses don't have a lot of working capital, most must do without the services of a good accountant in start-up or expansion phases, when they can do the most good. Large corporations often have the luxury of hiring financial experts skilled in all aspects of the business.

Here's a tip: Instead of hiring your own personal accountant, contact the State Department of Economic Development Office, or the Small Business Development Center (SBDC) or the local SCORE office near you. Many of these centers have accounting experts who will help you develop your own accounting and recordkeeping systems. They can also help you work through any accounting problems that you might encounter. If you don't have a local SBDC, contact your nearest Small Business Administration Office for advice. All SBDCs, SCORE Offices and SBA offices are listed on the SBA's web site at www.sba.gov.

USES OF MONEY

Few people have difficulty spending money. Every entrepreneur, however, should be familiar with and prepared for some very important uses of money. Below are typical uses of money.

Working capital

This money is used to buy inventory, pay salespersons, make lease payments, web site costs and handle unexpected costs until your Incoming Funds (revenues) can pay for all the Outgoing Funds (expenses).

Inventory

Because inventory can consume large amounts of working capital, make sure you buy the right amount of inventory. In retailing, for example, too-small quantities may lead to empty shelves and lost customers. Too large a stock, on the other hand, can raise your costs due to excess inventory and obsolete merchandise.

Excess inventory is a nonworking asset. As long as it sits on shelves, inventory ties up cash while producing no return. If your inventory is financed, you're actually paying someone for your stock to gather dust. To reduce inventory, some companies are turning to "just-in-time" systems. Instead of overstocking raw materials to ensure fast delivery, a just-in-time system shifts the burden to vendors through contracts that guarantee rapid shipments to fulfill customer orders.

Capital Equipment Purchases

Whether you start a business, buy one or get into a franchise, some of your largest expenses will be for capital equipment. When building your budget, remember that loans for machinery and capital equipment are generally easier to get, because they are secured by the equipment as collateral. These types of loans are based on the life of the equipment, but generally not for more than ten years. Certain technology costs are considered capital equipment purchases, but typically only if they cost over $5,000.

Research and Development

Ideas are the basis for most businesses, large and small. One idea may be enough to start an enterprise, but it isn't enough to maintain growth. The importance of improving existing products and developing new ones has never been more evident than it is today. Here are just a few examples or research and development in today's marketplace: The Campbell's Soup Company never stops developing new varieties and uses for their soups; Apple Computer constantly enhances and upgrades its product line; automobile companies are always involved in new product developments; even Hershey Chocolate eventually diversified into other candy products, building on the success of its original Hershey Bar to keep its share of an increasingly competitive market.

The lesson is that research and development is a continuing need for many businesses and that funds must be allocated or found for product development on a continuing basis.

Expansion

A good idea can't be held down. If a retailing idea is good in one location, two stores will probably be even better and ten stores will create a commanding purchasing situation. The same holds true in other marketing fields. If you've put together a hot selling organization for one line of products, chances are you can take on another line or two and be that much more successful.

Naturally, expansion always brings with it extra costs, but additional financing should be easy to come by if you have a successful record to show for your efforts.

Purchasing a Business

You never know when the opportunity to acquire a good company will come along, whether in your own business or in an allied field. Many entrepreneurs have made a career of going from success to success by keep keeping their eyes peeled for the right opportunity. Naturally, the better the record you establish in your main business, the easier it will be to get financing for a new acquisition.

CASH FLOW CONSIDERATIONS

Once you've established your business plans, it's time to set the facts and figures down on paper so you'll have a pretty good idea of how much money you'll need. Prospective lenders will definitely want to see some realistic figures before they even consider your request. They'll want to know how well you've budgeted your business as an indication of what kind of a risk (and rewards) you represent to them. In order to arrive at the right amount, you'll need to do some financial forecasting in the form of an income and expense forecast and cash flow projection.

Income and Expense Statement

It helps to think about the income and expense statement as the operating statement you would expect to see for your business at the end of a particular period, generally a year. For a new business, the forecast will be a prediction of revenues and expenses for the first year of operation. In either case, the analysis should answer the basic question of whether your business is going to make money. An example of an income and expense statement is shown in Figure 7.1.

Figure 7.1   Income and Expense Statement
AMERICAN PUBLISHING COMPANY
Year Ending December 31, 200X

INCOME	
20,000 books at $15.00 each	$300,000
EXPENSES	
Printing & Binding at $5.00 per book	$100,000
Wages and benefits for 2 employees	95,000
Depreciation on equipment	1,000
Overhead (power, light, heat, water)	2,000
Equipment repairs	500
Delivery & Freight	1,000
Marketing Expenses	1,500
Insurance	500
Rent	8,400
Interest on loans	200
Communications including Internet	2,400
Taxes	900
Accounting & Legal	800
Travel & Entertainment	2,000
Miscellaneous	1,200
TOTAL EXPENSES	**217,400**
NET PROFIT	**82,600**

Income

The first, and most uncertain, figure to estimate is income or sales. Because you need this figure to calculate your materials cost, you have to give your best estimate. Be conservative, it's better to underestimate than go overboard.

When estimating income, always keep in mind the following considerations:

- *Financing Costs.* If you use a line of credit to finance operations while waiting for your receivables to be paid, you are providing your clients with interest-free loans while paying interest to borrow against your line.
- *Opportunity Costs.*   If you had the money in hand, you could be investing it - either to earn interest or to make your company grow. But until your invoices are paid, your return is zero.
- *Administrative Costs.* The longer a receivable stays on the books, the more

you pay in rebilling costs, collection fees and related expenses.

To avoid such costs, you must establish an effective credit policy. Usually this includes methods for establishing and reviewing customer credit, service charges on over-due invoices, progress payments for products to be delivered over a period of time and positive collection efforts.

The most effective way to ensure timely payments is to keep in frequent and close contact with clients.

Expenses

Now prepare a list of expense items and your estimate of their costs-include such items as the following:

- *Labor*-This is the total amount of money you will be paying employees over the period of the statement.
- *Materials*-Depending on the type of business, this may include such items as office supplies, gift wrap, shipping supplies and so on.
- *Depreciation*-When you purchased any item that has a life span of three years or longer, the Internal Revenue Service normally will not allow you to treat the total cost of the item as a one-year expense. Rather, you are required to divide the cost of the item by the average life in terms of years assigned to the item. Thus, if an item costing $3,000 has a life span of three years, you can only write off $1,000 of the expense each year, for a three year period.
- *Marketing Expenses*-Estimate the amount of money you will spend to promote your business over the period of the statement. Be sure to include any web site costs as part of the marketing expenses.
- *Insurance*-Include total premiums paid on all of your different business insurance policies.
- *Utilities*-Include costs for heat, light, telephone, garbage removal, water, and so on.
- *Rent*-This includes the amount you pay the landlord or owner of your building.
- *Taxes*-Include all taxes your company will pay: various state and federal payroll taxes, sales taxes, and so on.
- *Interest on loans*-Include the total amount of interest you pay to those from whom you borrow
- *Professional* – Include fees and retainers paid to lawyers, accountants, engineers and so on.
- *Technology costs* – This includes any costs for web site development, new computers or software applications.

- *Miscellaneous costs* – This includes any expenses not covered by one of the above items.

Many times it is easier to split out the expenses as either fixed or variable expenses. Fixed expenses typically do not change over a period of time. Rent in an office building does not change month to month. Whereas materials or inventory may change with the different production or sales levels you may experience. This may be from a seasonal cycle or a response to your advertising campaign.

Managing Expenses

Managing the cash that leaves your company is just as important as regulating the funds that come into it. The first step is to put in to place an effective accounts payable system. You can set one up yourself or get an accountant to do it.

Payroll Costs

The costs of you and your full-time employees are essentially fixed - they remain the same whether business is good or bad, unless you have salespeople working on a commission basis. On the other hand, the salaries of part-time or temporary employees are variable costs from a cash flow standpoint, since they can be adjusted in response to business activity.

Tax Management

Business taxes include income, corporate, unemployment, Social Security (FICA), real estate sales and other categories that vary by locality. By managing your taxes wisely, you may be able to reduce quarterly tax payments when cash is scarce and increase them when business rebounds. To avoid penalties, however, always consult a qualified tax accountant before tinkering your with quarterly payments.

Net Profit

To arrive at the net profit on your income and expense forecast, add your expenses together and subtract that total from the income. Of course, if the expenses exceed the income, you will have a predicted net loss. If this is the case, you will need to reassess your figures and possibly your business idea to see if it really is workable.

Cash Flow Statements

A typical cash flow projection is illustrated in Figure 7.2. Cash flow statements are different than Income and Expense Statements in that you are trying to predict fluctuations in your cash flow, not if you are profitable. It is important when developing your cash flow statement to put the sales receipts and expenses in the category and month that they will be incurred. The cash flow statement will allow you to see when you will have an excess or a shortage of cash. Non-cash items are not included in the cash flow statement, like depreciation.

When creating a cash flow statement you can start with you initial cash investment and the expenses you will incur setting up the business. After that you will include the monthly sales receipts and expenses for the month that they occur. At the bottom of the statement, add together the beginning cash for that period and the sales receipts and subtract the expenses incurred. This will give you your ending cash for that period. If you have to order inventory in one month and pay for it the next month, you may have a shortage of cash for that particular month. This will allow you to draw on a line of credit or other back up funding method if needed.

The techniques we've discussed will not make all your cash flow problems disappear. No matter how well cash is managed, most firms experience periods when funds are tight and a line of credit is needed. However, taking an active role in the management of your company's cash flow ensures that you maximize profits by getting the most benefit from every dollar that comes in to or goes out of your business.

The important thing is to estimate, then go after and get, the money you'll actually need. Shooting for too little money is at least as unwise as asking for too much, and it's not necessarily easier to get lesser amount.

Figure 7.2 Sample Cash Flow Statement

	Starting	Month 1	Month 2		Month 12	Total
Beginning Cash						
Sale Receipts						
Fixed Expenses						
Rent						
Telephone						
Utilities						
Wages						
Variable Expenses						
Purchased Inventory						
Licenses & Permits						
Equipment						
Advertising						
Sales Commissions						
Delivery Costs						
Auto Expenses						
Travel & Entertainment						
Insurance						
Interest-mortgage						
Interest-loan						
Total Expenses						
Total Cash Flow (Excess or Deficit)						

Chapter 8

50+ Money Sources for Your Business

A key ingredient of business success is knowing how to use other people's money to finance a new or existing business. Obviously, if a company had an unlimited amount of money, there would be no need for outside financing. Administrators could lose endless amounts, spend as much as it wanted and not care how long it would take to make the business successful.

TWO TYPES OF FINANCING

Careful planning is the necessary ticket to successful financing or funding. In other words, it opens the door to reaching those people whose money you are going to use. Financing falls into two general categories: debt financing and equity financing.

Debt Financing

In it's most elementary form debt financing, is simply taking out a loan from a funding source and paying interest on it. Let's consider the example of a bank loan. Whether for use as working capital, a building mortgage, purchase of inventory or raw material, financing of a new venture or the purchase of a company truck are examples of debt financing. The bank provides the money and charges the borrower interest for the use of that money.

Debt financing relies heavily upon the individual or company's ability to pay back a loan. This can be in the form of putting up collateral or making available to the loan source assets equal or close to the value of the loan. It's like an insurance policy for the lender. That way, if the borrower defaults, the bank or loan agency is protected against loss. For example, collateral can be a first or second mortgage on a building, inventory, raw material, stocks, bonds, insurance or any other form of asset that can be assigned.

Debt financing can also rely on the firm's or individual's history. In the case of established companies and individuals that have a good credit history and rating, their history can be based simply on their reputation, size or the perception of their business in the community.

Equity Financing

Equity financing means obtaining funds in exchange for selling or giving up a part of interest in the business. Equity financing is not a loan; rather, it is the sale of part of your business. The purchaser relies upon is his or her belief that buying into the business is a good investment.

Equity financing has become very popular in recent years, especially in the biomedical, computer software and hardware and other high tech product development fields. These companies often have a product concept for which development costs can be considerable. Because they do not have the net worth, collateral or ability to repay any type of loan, they sell a portion of their business to raise money. Shares can be sold to the general public and listed on a national or local stock exchange. Common stock can also be privately held by shareholders and not publicly traded.

TRADITIONAL SOURCES

Sources of money can be divided between the traditional and nontraditional. We will start with a rundown of traditional sources.

Yourself

For the individual businessperson, the most logical place to look for financing is your own assets. These sources include money in bank accounts, certificates of deposit, stocks and bonds, cash value in insurance policies, real estate, home equity, value of hobby collections, automobiles, pension fund, Keogh or IRAs.

Obviously, if you had sufficient capital, there would be no need to turn to other sources for your needs. But, as noted before, to be successful in a business, most people must know how to use other people's money to finance the new or expanding business.

One word of caution: In today's fast moving economy, most of us have one or more credit cards. It is tempting to take advantage of the availability of money simply by using these cards. Remember, most credit card companies advance money at a much higher rate of interest than you would normally pay a bank or some other financing source. Equally important, although your monthly payments may appear to be small, because of the high interest, your debt compounds and rises quickly.

Family and Relatives

One common source of money is family and relatives. Too often, however, money can get in the way of good family relationships. Therefore, use extreme care in determining whether to approach a family member or relative.

One way you can avoid future problems and disagreements with relatives if they lend you money for your business is to have a written agreement. Spell out clearly the terms to which you and your relatives have agreed:

- Date of the loan
- Loan amount
- Date the loan will be repaid in full
- Dates of loan payments
- Frequently of payments: Monthly, quarterly, etc.
- Amount (percent) of interest
- Collateral, if any
- Signatures by both parties

One important note: It may be wise to make sure the relative from whom you are borrowing has notified his or her spouse. That way, you can ensure that no future problem arises due to any miscommunication.

Friends

There is the old adage, "don't mix business with pleasure." Quite frequently, however, friends represent an excellent source of money needed for a small business start-up or an ongoing business. When borrowing from friends, exercise the same caution and documentation as you would from relatives, to make sure that borrowing will not result in the loss of friendship or cause a serious rift to arise.

Your Own Company

If you already have an established company and are in need of money, one of the first places to turn is within the company itself. An established company or business has several options available. These include taking a first or second mortgage on any real estate or property that it owns; borrowing money against machinery or hard assets such as equipment or motor vehicles; or borrowing against a pension fund or inventory that is considered liquid.

Pledging Accounts Receivable   A common method by which companies can obtain a loan is by pledging the firm's accounts receivable in return for a loan. This means that your receivables are pledged or turned over to the bank or loan company that makes the loan. Then, as the receivables are paid, the firm deducts a certain amount of each payment until the loan is paid. Essentially, what the bank or loan company is doing is using your accounts receivable as collateral against the loan.

Factoring   Factoring is another way of using your receivables to raise badly needed cash. In factoring, one goes to a factoring company, which actually buys your accounts receivables.

Assume, for example, that you have $50,000 in accounts receivables and it is a particularly slow time of the year in which you have very little cash flow. The factor will buy your $50,000 in receivables. Possibly they will give you $30,000 or $40,000 for them. The factor then owns the receivables. The amount of discount that the factor takes depends on such things as how old your accounts receivable are, who owes you the money, what you sell, how long you have been in business and so on.

You can find a listing of factors in the Yellow Pages. You can also get a list of such companies from your banker.

Commercial Banks

Banks are the standard lending organizations for business. They represent the largest single source for loans and financing. Their basic business is to provide and manage money for individuals, businesses and organizations. Commercial banks are the main lender for the Small Business Administration.

Interest on loans is commercial bank's main source of income. The amount of interest they charge is based upon two factors: the size and history of the customer and the risk the bank will take in providing the loan.

Interest charges are almost always based upon some factor of the prime interest rate, the lowest rate banks charge their most favored customers. These customers are generally large companies and businesses.

Banks will charge smaller and riskier (in their judgment) customers an interest rate over and above the prime rate. For example, if the customer is a small business with one or two loan experiences, the bank may charge two points over the prime rate. This means is that if the prime rate is eight percent, the small business customer may have to pay ten percent for his or her loan.

Savings and Loan Organizations

These are like banks, but are organized under a different type of charter. Originally established to facilitate the lending of money for home mortgages, they have gradually evolved into full-service banking operations. There are some government restrictions on where and how they can operate as compared to commercial banks. Like banks, their charge for loans is based on the prime rate or some variation of it.

During 1991 and 1992 the Savings and Loan industry was rocked by a great number of scandals involving poor-risk loans. As a result, the remaining saving and loans are taking a very careful look at any business loan application. Many now require any loan be backed up by an equivalent amount of collateral.

Loan Companies

Loan companies, which exist in most U.S. cities and communities, represent one of the largest sources of money in the country. Unlike banks, which obtain from many different sources, loan companies have to rely upon their own capital or raising money, just as other businesses do. Thus their interest rates are usually higher. In some instances, they can be several percentage points above the prime rate.

Loan companies are considered collateral lenders, that is, they rely heavily upon the ability of the borrower's ability to back up every dollar of the loan with a pledge or assignment of some assets. For example, a borrower may have to pledge accounts receivable, put up the mortgage on the company's building, or assign the value of an insurance policy, stocks or bonds.

Loan companies often have different operating policies, and the interest rates they charge may vary as much as five percent from one firm to another. It is therefore prudent to shop around before you settle on a particular loan company. For a listing of loan companies in your area, check the Yellow Pages.

Insurance Companies, Pension Funds and Unions

Existing companies can tap these three sources of money for direct loans or investment purposes. All three are generally interested only in making loans of substantial size, and so would not be interested in making loans to small start-up businesses. Usually their loans are tied to some form of equity ownership. For example, in Minneapolis, the country's largest shopping mall was funded primarily out of a teachers' union pension fund. Here, the pension fund financed the building mortgage. For this, they received a substantial interest in the ownership of the mall.

Credit Unions

A significant source of funding can be found in the credit unions. Credit unions were established with two objectives: to provide a savings vehicle for its members and to be a lender to members in need of loans, primarily for purchasing automobiles and appliances purchases or emergency financial needs.

In recent years, credit unions have expanded their lending operations to include non-members and investments outside of traditional financial investments. In the past, credit unions would only invest in U. S. Treasury bills and notes, certificates of deposit, and highly rated corporate bonds. Now, they seek out other investments, such as new company start-ups and direct company loans, where they can realize a much higher rate of return or actually secure an equity interest in the company to which they are making the loan.

Micro Enterprise Programs

There are two types of micro enterprise programs: SBA funded microloan programs and private micro enterprise programs. Both private and SBA programs provide very small loans to start-up, newly established, or growing small business concerns. Under the SBA microloan program, the SBA makes funds available to nonprofit community based lenders (intermediaries) which, in turn, make loans to eligible borrowers in amounts up to a maximum of $35,000. The average loan size is about $10,500. Applications are submitted to the local intermediary and all credit decisions are made on the local level.

Each lender has its own lending and credit requirements. However, business owners contemplating application for a microloan should be aware that both programs will generally require some type of collateral, and the personal guarantee of the business owner. The SBA program also requires its intermediaries to provide business based training and technical assistance to its borrowers.

Small Business Investment Companies

These are privately owned companies licensed and insured by the U.S. Small Business Administration to provide capital to small firms. Small Business Investment Companies usually focus on specific industries such as medically-oriented high technology enterprises, or agricultural, manufacturing or real estate companies.

Several Small Business Investment Companies exist in each state; to find them, contact the nearest Office of Small Business Administration or obtain a listing of them for your area from the U.S. Department of Commerce or your local Congressional representative. They are also available on the Internet at www.sba.gov.

Small Business Innovation Research Fund

The SBIR program is funded by 11 federal agencies that publish a list of specific program needs, problems or opportunities. The agencies invest small amounts of money in the concept and feasibility stages of development. The second phase is developing a prototype. In the final phase of moving the product to the commercial market is handled by non-SBIR funding sources. More information on this program can be found at **www.sba.gov**. Some examples of federal agencies that participate in this program are:

- Department of Defense
- Department of Health & Human Services
- NASA
- Department of Energy
- National Science Foundation
- Department of Agriculture
- Department of Transportation
- Department of Education

Certified Development Companies

The SBA 504 Certified Development Company (CDC) Program provides growing businesses with long-term, fixed-rate financing for major fixed assets, such as land and buildings. A Certified Development Company is a nonprofit corporation set up to contribute to the economic development of its community. CDCs work with the SBA and private-sector lenders to provide financing to small businesses. There are about 270 CDCs nationwide. Each CDC covers a specific geographic area. The funds in this program are used for:
Business district revitalization
Expansion of exports
Expansion of minority business development
Rural development
Enhanced economic competition
Restructuring because of federally mandated standards or policies
Changes necessitated by federal budget cutbacks
Expansion of small business concerns owned and controlled by veterans
Expansion of small business concerns owned and controlled by women

To locate a CDC in your area, go to: http://www.sba.gov/gopher/Local-Information/Certified-Development-Companies/

Government Assistance Programs

Some government program, because they are supported by public funds, are aimed at solving a particular problem. Most programs are either loans, grants, contract awards, or credits. Contract awards are for specific products that the government uses and credits are generally tax incentives to companies for providing new jobs or economic growth for a specific area. The following are some organizations to contact for more information:

- Local Economic Development Associations
- Local Enterprise Zones
- State Office of Economic Development (may have different name in different states)
- State Business Development Fund (may be called Finance Authority, Industrial Revenue Bond Funds, Board of Investments)
- State Procurement Technical Assistance Centers

Import and Export Financing

If your company is doing business globally, you probably need help with import and export financing. There are a few different places that offer financing for this type of activity.

The SBA has an International Trade Loan and an Export Working Capital Loan Programs. To learn more go to the SBA web site at www.sba.gov.

The Export-Import Bank also has a variety of programs to help small businesses export more products overseas. The first is a short term insurance program that allows the small business to offer credit terms to the foreign customer. This is important because many foreign buyers expect the United States business to offer this service. This program protects the exporter from payment default of the foreign customer. The second program is a Medium Term Export Credit Insurance. This program allows the exporter to offer credit terms of 1-7 years to the foreign customer. The Ex-Im Bank will insure against default of the foreign customer in case of commercial or political risk. The third program is a Working Capital Guarantee program that allows commercial lenders to make working capital loans to U. S. exporters for export-related expenses by substantially reducing the risks associated with these loans.

Private Investors

These individuals or groups make investments and loans, usually in exchange for an equity interest in a company. They work with existing concerns and new business start-ups. The objective of and the size of funds available from private investors vary widely. Some, for example, confine their activities to high technology firms, while others, may invest or lend money to retailers.

Generally speaking, private investors only want to make an investment in the company. They want no part of the day-to-day activities of the company, nor are they interested in becoming involved with ongoing business decisions. Some limit their participation to under $50,000; others may consider only companies in need of a half million dollars or more. Most can be found through local bankers, accountants or lawyers or your local newspaper's Sunday classified advertising pages.

ACE-Net was started by the Small Business Administration, but as of April 2000, the organization has become an independent not-for-profit. ACE-Net provides private investors and entrepreneurs a way of finding each other through an Internet database. Currently the 358 active investors and 328 entrepreneur company listings. ACE-Net is for companies that are not sole-proprietorships, partnerships, development stage companies or investment companies. To find a local contact for ACE-Net go to https://ace-net.sr.unh.edu/pub/carl.htm?TYPE=wel.

Venture Capitalists

A form of private investor is the venture capitalist. This individual or group almost always provides funding for an equity or ownership interest in the firm. The venture capitalist is usually interested in high-technology, high growth or technology-related new business start-ups. Thus, they are concerned primarily with companies that are developing a new product and that usually will not have access to traditional money sources.

Ventures capitalists are like private investors in that they generally will not take an active role in the management or everyday affairs of the company they are providing funds. Their role can be passive, although they will typically require that they join the company's board of directors. Some venture capital companies have changed over the past few years. Many are bringing more to companies than they have in the past. Some venture capitalists will help high growth companies find experienced high level managers or contacts to potential customers. Most venture capitalists are looking for a minimum of 30% return on their money within 5 years.

New Markets Venture Capital Companies (NMVCC) are regulated and overseen by the SBA to make sure the public policy objectives are being met. The NMVCC is eligible for grant and operational assistance from the SBA. At least 80% of the NMVCCs investments must be in smaller enterprises by SBA guidelines, in low-income geographic areas as defined by the SBA and must have equity capital investments, including common stock, preferred stock or some subordinated debt structures.

Leasing Companies

The role of leasing companies and organizations has traditionally been tied to providing motor vehicles for individuals and companies. Gradually this role has changed. Leasing companies began moving into fleet leasing, consisting of up to hundreds of automobiles, trucks, cargo carriers, buses, and airplanes. Many have even taken over the financing of cargo and passenger vessels.

In recent years, these same leasing companies have further diversified their operations; they are now known to pay for the purchase of new inventory and provide money for leasehold improvements such as decorating and remodeling. They may even provide money for working capital. Since leasing companies derive their income from the use of capital, many have recently moved into many areas previously considered the domain of banks and loan companies.

Government Grants

The SBA does not have grants available for individuals who want to start, operate or expand a small business. Although the infomercials are misleading, the federal government does not have grant money available for small businesses. Grants must be approved by Congress and included as part of annual federal budget. As of the writing of this book, the state of the federal budget and most state's budgets are in the process of being cut. Most of the grant funds available are for other government organizations or not-for-profit programs. If you would like to check out grants that are available, you can do a search of program at the Catalog of Federal Domestic Assistance web site at www.cfda.gov.

There are some grant programs available to small businesses including the Small Business Innovation Research program (discussed earlier). But most of these grants are for developing new technologies.

The best place to look for grant money is through organizations that either have contests or cash prizes. One example may be a business plan competition offered by a local financial institution or magazine with cash awards.

In looking for grants, it never hurts to call your local city hall, county offices, or state department of economic development to see if they have any new programs for their area. Some government organizations may be trying to increase specific types of businesses, like women-owned or manufacturing businesses in their community.

NONTRADITIONAL SOURCES

Non-traditional sources are unlimited in number and type, but you need to be creative to acquire the necessary funding from them for your start-up or expanding business.

Customers

Customers or potential customers can be an excellent source of funding. Consider the following examples: Two engineers worked together at the same company. On their own time, they develop a new plastic, the manufacturing of which requires a large capital investment. When used as raw material, their plastic, is one-third the cost of the product companies or customers are currently using. The engineers contact a large potential user, who realizes that the new plastic can reduce her raw material costs significantly. Subsequently, she lends the two engineers the money necessary to start their own business. In return for her investment, the user receives a contract assuring her company of getting 75 percent of the manufacturing output of the new plastic.

Another example is that of a cosmetologist who wants to open her own salon. In conversations with a customer, it turns out that the customer likewise wants to have her own business. The customer invests in the salon and the two form a partnership. The cosmetologist manages the salon and the other employees; her partner participated in the day-to-day affairs of the salon handling bookkeeping, advertising and customer service.

Suppliers

Suppliers can be a great source of funding because they can often be assured of becoming the principal supplier to a customer they've helped; this holds true especially in highly competitive fields.

Suppliers will often provide supplemental equipment that is necessary for use with the products they provide. For example, food wholesalers will often provide display cases, shelving and other equipment.

For example, let's say a bakery-delicatessen in a major city decided it was necessary to open a second location to accommodate customers who had moved to another, growing residential area. To finance the expansion, the owners contact their major suppliers. A milling company advances them $100,000 at an interest rate substantially below prevailing market rates to purchase ovens. For this consideration, the bakery owners promise to buy from the supplier a minimum of 75 percent of their flour for the next three years. The owners also obtain funds from their deli meat supplier to purchase to purchase their new refrigeration deli display cases.

Employees

Typically raising money from employees happens in Employee Stock

Option Plans in larger companies. But raising money from employees has become more common lately when an owner wants to sell their portion of the business. Instead of an outsider coming in to run the business, management can do a buy-out or the employees can try to raise funds by themselves to keep the business. If you are a small company, this may not be an alternative for raising cash. Sometimes when you allow employees to become partners, they think they can create more of the vision for the company going forward. There may be more problems with employees not all agreeing with your plans or ideas.

Bartering

Bartering is the act of trading products or services with another company or individual. Bartering allows you to receive products or services that you need for your business in addition to conserving your cash. In using this method of financing, look for businesses where you can benefit from each other's customer base or product or service offerings. For example, an advertising firm could produce a small radio campaign for a computer company in exchange for a new computer for the advertising company. One thing to remember when bartering is that the transaction is viewed as income by the IRS.

Joint Ventures

Joint ventures are partnerships where each party is an active part of the transaction. Joint ventures can help to keep costs down for each company by sharing the work load and splitting the expenses. For example, two financial planners or accountants can share office space and a receptionist to help control costs. This type of sharing of expenses is very common in beauty salons. Typically in a salon, the hair stylist "rents" a chair and pays a portion of the receptionist, utilities and marketing expenses of the salon. Joint ventures can be small agreements or larger agreements for complex research and development efforts. Joint ventures are really only limited to a business owner's creativity and negotiation skills.

Local Development Companies

These organizations have been formed to attract new business to particular areas. They are frequently established in rural communities and small towns. Usually they are made up of local banks, real estate firms and local business association members who band together to bring in new industry. These nonprofit institutions are in a position to offer land and buildings, even capital. Local development companies often obtain their funds from unusual sources; for example, one in Minnesota is funded through a local board of education.

Franchising

Offering your business concept as a franchise to other entrepreneurs is one way of expanding your business and raising some additional financing. Franchising is not a start-up funding source, but one that can be used in expansion or growth. Franchising allows you to profit from sharing your secrets to success with others. To be successful at franchising your business concept, you need to identify and understand exactly what processes make you successful and how can you train someone else on these procedures. The paperwork to set up a franchise for your business concept can be complex. To learn more about franchising, contact the International Franchise Association.

Licensing

Licensing is like franchising except you are selling the rights for someone to duplicate a technology process or service system for a fee. Licensing is easier to set up than franchising. Since licensing is specific to a certain technology or process, the number of potential buyers of the license may be more limited than franchising. In the past many third world countries purchase licenses for technological advances that would take too long and too much money to develop on their own. Licensing is the transfer of specific knowledge for a stated amount of time. It is very important to be clear about the technology or process that you are selling. To learn more contact experts in your field to help you identify possible processes that may be licensable.

Business Incubators

From the National Business Incubation Association: "Incubators nurture young firms, helping them to survive and grow during the start-up period when they are most vulnerable. Incubators provide hands-on management assistance, access to financing and orchestrated exposure to critical business or technical support services. They also offer entrepreneurial firms shared office services, access to equipment, flexible leases and expandable space — all under one roof. An incubation program's main goal is to produce successful graduates — businesses that are financially viable and freestanding when they leave the incubator, usually in two to three years."

Incubators are much like venture capitalists in that some are specific to an industry while others concentrate on a mix of businesses. Businesses that are in incubators today are generally ones with new or innovative technologies.

To find an incubator in your area, go to the National Business Incubation web site at www.nbia.org.

Cash Advances for Visa and MasterCard Receipts

Typically to be eligible your business needs to be processing over $5,000 in Visa or MasterCard receipts per month. Lenders will take a portion of the on going credit card receipts as a form of payment on the loan. Normally there are no up front costs, fixed payments or fixed time frame for repayment.

Purchase Order Financing

Purchase order financing is used in cases where your suppliers want to be paid up front and your customers want to pay you in 30-60 days. There is no cash flow during manufacturing, delivery or until invoices are paid. The funding source will pay your supplier directly reserving your own cash to pay your other business expenses.

Advertising for Money

You can actively seek funding by running a display advertisement in the business section or under the appropriate heading in the classified ads of your local newspaper. Specify the amount of money needed and the type of business for which it will be used. Confidentiality for both parties can be maintained through the use of a post office box or newspaper box number.

An example of an advertisement recently placed in the business opportunity section of a newspaper's classified advertising pages is shown in Figure 8.1. In this ad, the party seeking the loan was interested in finding someone who would make a straight $50,000 loan. Another alternative could have offered an opportunity to buy into the business, as shown in the sample ad in Figure 8.2.

Figure 8-1

Business Investment Opportunity
Rapidly growing retail store seeks additional capital of up to $50,000 for expansion purposes. Low risk investment with 10% interest return on your investments. For information write P.O. Box 27612, Minneapolis, MN 55426 or call 612-957-3344.

Figure 8-2

Business Investment **Opportunity** Rapidly growing retail store seeks financial partner interested in investing up to $50,000 in exchange for an equity ownership in the store. For additional information write P.O. Box 27612 Minneapolis, MN 55426 or call 612-957-3344

Another alternative for money for small businesses is that which is provided by the U. S. Small Business Administration, which will be discussed in the next chapter.

Chapter 9

Small Business Administration Programs

The Small Business Administration (SBA) was created in 1953 through Congress's passage of the Small Business Act. It was established to help create and maintain successful small businesses by offering financing, training, assistance and advocacy programs for small business.

The Small Business Administration programs have assisted many individuals starting and forming new businesses, as well as owners of existing small businesses. The SBA provides assistance in a wide variety of areas: finance, marketing, production, human resource management, loans, export, government procurement, innovation and research, women's business ownership, minority business ownership, education, and training. It is also the government's principal arm for disaster assistance and maintains four Disaster Assistance offices.

Headquartered in Washington, D.C., the SBA has ten regional offices and approximately 100 district, branch and post-of-duty offices in all 50 states, the District of Columbia, Guam, Puerto Rico and the Virgin Islands. The head of the SBA is appointed by the President and confirmed by the Senate.

The SBA has a number of major partners in providing assistance. These include: SCORE, Small Business Development Centers (SBDC), Small Business Institutes (SBI), and Business Information Centers (BIC)

SCORE Association

SCORE is made up of executives from both small and large businesses, who volunteers their time to provide free counseling to small business and individuals interested in starting small businesses. They also conduct regular seminars and workshops on various topics. SCORE has 390 chapters and 270 satellite offices across the country. They can be found by going to the SBA website at www.sba.gov.

Small Business Development Centers

SBDCs are a cooperative effort of local, state and federal governments. The bulk of the funding comes from the SBA. There are approximately 900 SBDCs and sub-centers throughout the country. Almost all of them are affiliated with colleges, universities, or vocational technical training schools or other educational institutions. SBDCs provide a wide range of assistance to new business start-ups and operating small businesses. They offer assistance in counseling, market studies, business plan writing, advertising and public relations, and financial analysis. In addition, they offer courses on setting up and operating small businesses.

Small Business Institutes

SBIs are also a cooperative effort between local, state and federal governments. Located at colleges and universities, they use students enrolled in business classes together with faculty members to provide assistance in the form of counseling, material and technical assistance, research studies and other specialized activities, to individuals and small businesses.

Business Information Centers

BICs provide high-tech hardware, software and telecommunications in conjunction with SCORE counseling services. There are operational sites all around the country.

In addition to its counseling and educational services, the SBA publishes a wide range of periodicals and literature to assist small business and individuals thinking about going into their own small businesses. These publications are available on the SBA website at www.sba.gov.

THE SBA GUARANTEED LOAN PROGRAM

The SBA is best known for its activities in the field of lending and providing financial assistance to small businesses. Clouding these activities is a common misconception that the SBA is like a bank, lending money directly to individuals and businesses. Nothing could be further from the truth.

The SBA does, however, provide a wide range of lending and financial assistance activities. We'll discuss many of these functions. For detailed information on each of them, you should contact your nearest SBA office or their web site at www.sba.gov.

The SBA offers several categories of loans, most which fall under the SBA Guaranteed Loan Program. There are a number of reasons why a company or individual turns to the SBA:

- The small business owner needs more time than a traditional bank will allow to pay back a loan.
- The borrower lacks sufficient collateral
- The borrower is the owner of a start-up company, and lacks the business experience required by most banks.

SBA loans are available to existing and start-up companies alike. There are no restrictions as to the number of SBA loans a company or individual may have, as long as the SBA's exposure does not exceed $750,000. For example, a company can have three different SBA loans, all from different banks or lending agencies, provided the total amount of the loans is not greater than $750,000.

Under the Small Business Act, all loans made under the various SBA loan programs must be of "sound value or so secured as to reasonably ensure repayment." This means that the individual or company asking for the loan must demonstrate good business judgment, have made some equity investment in the company, and have some collateral to back up the loan.

With regard to providing SBA loans, the agency is interested in encouraging new business start-ups and providing for the continuation in business of small businesses in need of financing.

Qualifying for an SBA Loan

To qualify for a SBA loan, a business must show that it is a small business that is independently owned and not part of some other large company or organization. It cannot be a major or the dominant firm in the industry. And most important, the small business must show that has the ability to repay the loan.

Collateral Requirements Like all lending agencies, the SBA generally attempts to secure its loans with as much collateral as possible. Collateral is defined by Webster as "designating of security given as a pledge for the fulfillment of an obligation; hence secured or guaranteed by property." This can include a wide variety of items such as accounts receivable, stocks, bonds, cash value in life insurance, equipment, fixtures, raw materials, inventory, automobiles, trucks, furniture or real estate. Frequently, the collateral put up for the loan is exactly what the loan is used for. For example, to purchase machinery or add inventory the machinery or inventory becomes the collateral.

This does not mean that, for every dollar that they guarantee in a loan, the SBA requires that a dollar of collateral be made available to them. It does mean that the individual or company making a loan application must make every reasonable effort to secure the loan with as much collateral as possible.

Equity Requirements The SBA also requires that loan applicants have a sufficient amount of his or her own equity in the business. In other words, the party seeking the loan, must at one point have invested a reasonable amount of their own personal money in the business. Although there is no clear definition of what the amount of equity is, it is expected that applicants will invest a fair amount of their own capital if starting a new business, or if it is an ongoing business, that they would have made an earlier investment of their own money or assets.

What is a Small Business?

In order to qualify for an SBA loan, an existing business must be qualified as "small" under the SBA size and standard guidelines. The standards differ by industry and may be measured in terms of dollars or number of employees.

These standards are described below:

- *Wholesale.* The average number of employees per pay period for the preceding 12 months may not exceed 100 (this includes part-time and temporary employees).
- *Retail.* The average annual receipts for the last three years must be less than $3.5 million.
- *Service Company.* The average annual receipts for the last three years must be less than $3.5 million, with the exception of real estate agents, who must have average annual receipts of less than $1million for the last three years.
- *Construction.* The average annual receipts for the last three years must be less than $17 million, except for certain dredging and cleanup activities. Special trade construction operations, that is, operations that work in a special construction vocational activity, are limited to the last three years' sales average of not more than $7 million.
- *Farming.* The average annual receipts for the last three years must be less than $500,000.

The preceding standards are not, however, cast in concrete. Certain types of businesses may exceed these limits, yet be accepted for a loan. If you do not meet the criteria for your specific industry, contact your nearest SBA office to determine whether a variance will be accepted.

Exclusions The following types of businesses are not eligible to receive loans under any of the SBA's loan programs:

- Nonprofit organizations
- Mini Storage companies
- Radio and television stations
- Film, record and tape distributors
- Real property held primarily for sale or investment
- Illegal gambling activities
- Businesses involved in speculation

For additional types of firms that are excluded from participating in the SBA loan program, contact you local SBA office. Also, individuals who are currently in prison, on probation or on parole for a serious offense may not make apply for a loan.

Applying for a Guaranteed Loan

The SBA has regular procedures for applying for loans, and these usually take anywhere from a day or two up to a couple of months depending on the complexity of the deal. To apply for an SBA guaranteed loan, the small business borrower must go through several steps and complete a number of SBA forms and applications. To complete these forms, the borrower needs to have all of the information found in the checklist shown in figure 9.1, and must complete the forms listed in Appendix A.

Once approved, the loan is made through a bank or an authorized banking agency. Although the loan is actually supplied by the bank, the SBA operates as an insurance company for the loan; in the event that the borrower defaults on the loan, the SBA will guarantee the payment of up to 80 percent of the outstanding balance of the loan.

Loans under the Guaranteed Loan Program are made in conjunction with three parties: the SBA, the small business borrowing the funds and the private lender. In most cases the private lender is a bank. The flow chart in Figure 9.2 shows the SBA guaranteed loan application process.

Figure 9.2

1. The Small Business seeking the loan submits its loan application to the bank or lending agency.
2. Lending agency forwards loan application to the SBA, together with its credit analysis.
3. SBA approves of the loan application.
4. Lending agency closes or concurs with the loan.
5. Lender and borrower agree on a repayment program.
6. Small Business borrower receives funds from the lender.
7. Small Business borrower begins making repayment of the loan with interest.

Interest Rates Two rate structures are available for SBA guaranteed loans: fixed and variable. Variable rate loans can be adjusted monthly, quarterly, semiannually or annually and float with the prime rate. Fixed-rate loans do not change during the life of the loan. The maximum allowable rate for both types of loans is 2-3/4 percent over the prime rate for loans of seven years and longer, and 2-1/4 percent over the prime rate for loans up to seven years. The prime rate is the minimum New York prime rate as published in the Wall Street Journal.

Maturity The length of a loan is determined by the use of the loan proceeds. Working capital loans are generally limited to seven years. Loans for machinery and capital equipment are based on the life of the equipment but not generally over ten years. Real estate loans have a maximum maturity of 25 years.

Uses of Loan Proceeds SBA loans can be used by existing or start-up businesses and can be used for the purchase of an existing business. This means that the individual or company taking out a SBA loan can use the proceeds for working capital, to purchase inventory, plant and equipment, raw material, goods in process, finished goods, adding labor, making payments for accounts payable and for almost any expense or asset need of the enterprise.

Repayment Terms

Once an SBA loan application is made and approved, representatives of the business meet with their bank lending officer to discuss various repayment points. These include repayment terms of the loan, commencement date for repayment, length of the loan period and schedule for repayment.

These points are determined by each particular business. Factors taken into consideration include projected sales and earnings, use of the loan proceeds, business equity, management and an analysis of the small business and its operation. Indeed, the SBA and the bank, or lending agency are not interested in setting a repayment program that will impair the stability of the business and place the proceeds of the loan and the business in jeopardy.

The SBA forms required for any loan are shown in Figure 9.3.

Checklist 9.4 Small Business Administration Loan Forms

1. Application for Loan: SBA form 4, 4I
2. Statement of Personal History: SBA form 912
3. Personal Financial Statement: SBA form 413
4. Detailed, signed Balance Sheet and Profit & Loss
   Statements current (within 90 days of application) and last three (3) fiscal years Supplementary Schedules required on Current Financial Statements.
5. Detailed one (1) year projection of Income & Finances
   (please attach written explanation as to how you expect to achieve same).
6. A list of names and addresses of any subsidiaries and affiliates, including concerns in which the applicant holds a controlling (but not necessarily a majority), interest and other concerns that may be affiliated by stock ownership, franchise, proposed merger or otherwise with the applicant.
7. Certificate of Doing Business (If a corporation, stamp corporate seal on SBA form 4 section 12).
8. By Law, the Agency may not guarantee a loan if a business can obtain funds on reasonable terms from a bank or other private source. A borrower therefore must first seek private financing. A company must be independently owned and operated, not dominant in its field and must meet certain standards of size in terms of employees or annual receipts. Loans cannot b made to speculative businesses, newspapers, or businesses engaged in
   gambling.

   Applicants for loans must also agree to comply with SBA regulation that there will be no discrimination in employment or services to the public, based on race, color, religion, national origin, sex or marital status.
9. Signed Business Federal Income Tax Returns for previous three (3) year.
10. Signed Personal Federal Income Tax Returns of principals for previous three (3) years.
11. Personal Resume including business experience of each principal.
12. Brief history of the business and its problems:
   Include an explanation of why the SBA loan is needed and how it will help the business.
13. Copy of Business Lease (or note from landlord giving terms of proposed lease.
14. For purchase of an existing business:
   a. Current Balance Sheet and Profit & Loss Statement of business to be purchased.

b. Previous two (2) years Federal Income Tax Returns of the business.
c. Propose Bill of Sale Including: Terms of Sale.
d. Asking Price with schedule of:
   1. Inventory
   2. Machinery & Equipment
   3. Furniture & Fixtures

Copies of each of these forms is found on the SBA web site at http://www.sba.gov/library/forms.html.

One important element that is not provided for in any formal format or form that generally must be submitted when applying for an SBA loan is a Business Plan.

SPECIALIZED GUARANTEED SBA LOAN PROGRAMS

Pollution Control Loans

These types of loans are offered through the guaranteed loan program. They must meet the same credit criteria and conditions as the regular guaranteed loans. The maximum amount is $1 million, or up to 85 percent of the needed amount of money. Proceeds must be used to finance the planning, design or installation of a pollution control facility which is defined as real or personal property that is likely to help prevent, reduce, abate or control noise, air or water pollution.

International Trade Loans

Also offered through the guaranteed loan program, these loans to help small businesses finance their export or overseas business. A firm can seek funds through this program if, for example, it needs working capital to purchase equipment or to finance facility expansion in order to take care of their overseas sales. The program also helps firms buying or selling products overseas. Frequently, payment by the overseas buyer is made by a letter of credit, which tells the supplier that they are guaranteed payment, since the money has been deposited in a bank.
    This letter of credit cannot, however, be turned into cash by the small business until shipment is actually made of whatever has been ordered. It may take up to several months for a small business to produce the order; thus, working capital is needed to finance the business during this timeframe. This is where the International Trade Loan comes into play. These loans are limited to a maximum of $1 million or up to 85 percent of the needed funds, to a maximum of $250,000 for working capital.

OTHER SBA LOAN PROGRAMS

In addition to the previously discussed guaranteed loans, the SBA offers a number of other specific loan programs, which fall into several different categories:

- SBA short term loans
- Seasonal line of credit
- Small general contractor
- Export revolving line
- Handicapped assistance
- Veterans and disabled veterans
- Development company loan program
- Micro loan program

SBA Short-Term Loans

Contract Loan Program The contract loan program provides working capital to those companies in need of money to meet, complete and fulfill the obligations of a short term contract. To qualify, a business must have been in operation for 12 months or more preceding the date of application. The loan amount is limited to the cash requirement for the labor and material portion of the contract only.

For example, a clothing manufacturer may have received a contract to produce 25,000 pair of pants. The contract is between the small business textile manufacturer and a leading nationwide discount store chain. To complete the contract, the producer needs to purchase the cloth material from which the pants will be made. Having exhausted his or her alternatives for raising the necessary capital to purchase the raw material, the producer can apply for such a loan from the SBA. Each loan of this nature applies to a specific contract that the borrower has.

Seasonal Line of Credit

The seasonal line of credit is used to finance working capital needs arising from the seasonal upswings of a business. Typical uses are to build up inventory and pay for increased labor costs resulting from seasonal trends. The SBA will guarantee as much as 85 percent of the loan up to $750,000. For loans of up to $155,000, the agency can guarantee up to 90 percent of the principal. Finally, the term of the seasonal line of credit loan cannot be more then 12 months from the date of the SBA's first disbursement.

These loans are available under the guaranty loan program and must meet the same criteria as other SBA guaranteed loans.

Small General Contractor Loans

The Small General Contractor Loan is a short-term program designed to finance residential and commercial construction or rehabilitation for resale. The applicant must be a construction contractor; a company that subcontracts all work is not eligible. The SBA can guarantee as much as 85 percent of the loan up to $750,000. The maximum guaranty for loans up to $155,000 is 90 percent.

The loan maturity cannot be more than 36 months plus a reasonable estimate of the time it takes to complete the construction or renovation. Principal repayment may be required in a single payment when the project is sold.

For such loans, three documents are required:

1. A letter from the mortgage lender doing business in the area, affirming that permanent mortgage financing for qualified purchasers of comparable real estate is normally available in the project's area.
2. A letter from an independently licensed real estate broker with three years' experience on the project area. The letter must state whether a market for the proposed structure exists and whether it is compatible with other buildings in the neighborhood.
3. A letter from an independent architect, appraiser or engineer, confirming availability of the construction inspection and certification at intervals during the project.

Export Revolving Line

The Export Revolving Line provides funds for the manufacture or purchase of goods or services for export purposes or to penetrate foreign markets. This loan has a revolving feature, in that multiple lines of credit may exist simultaneously as long as they do not exceed $750,000 together. One qualification is that the firm applying for the loan must have been in business for a period of 12 months prior to the loan application date.

Handicapped Assistance Loans

The SBA also offers a number of direct loans for which it directly disburses funds. These loans are available to handicapped individuals and public or private nonprofit sheltered workshops.

First is the handicapped assistance loan, known as the HAL. There are two types of HAL loans: HAL-1 provides financial assistance to public or private nonprofit sheltered workshops; and HAL-2 provides financial assistance for small businesses owned 100percent by a handicapped person. The handicapped individual must actively participate in managing the business; businesses owned by an absentee handicapped owner are not eligible.

The interest rate on both of these loans is 3% and the maximum amount of the loan is limited to $150,000.

Vietnam-Era and Disabled Veteran programs

Another SBA direct loan program provides financial assistance for Vietnam-era and disabled veterans. Private financing and guaranty loans must be used if available. In order to qualify, at least 51 percent of the business must be owned by a qualifying veteran or veterans.

These loans have a maximum ceiling or loan amount of $150,000. To be eligible, Vietnam-era veterans must have served for more than 180 days between August 5, 1964 and May 7, 1975 and must not have received a dishonorable discharge. Veterans with 30 percent or more compensable disability or who have received a disability discharge are considered disabled veterans.

Collateral requirements are not nearly as strict for these programs as for other SBA loans. The SBA must be satisfied that loans are of sufficiently sound value or reasonably secured to ensure repayment. A side benefit of the SBA involvement with veterans is that they will provide special assistance and training as it applies to their specific business. This training is done in conjunction with a lender, if one is available.

Development Company Loan Program

This program operates in two different areas. One is the Local Development Company or 502 program. This type of loan is made to a local development company consisting of at least 25 stockholders. The loan is made by a participating bank and guaranteed by the SBA. For more information on local development companies, see Chapter 7. The other is the Certified Development Company loan, or 504 program. The purpose of this program is to help communities stimulate the growth and expansion of small businesses within a defined area of operation.

- Proceeds of Certified Development Company loans may be used for:
- Purchasing of existing buildings
- Purchasing land and land improvements
- Construction
- Purchasing machinery and equipment
- Paying interest on interim financing
- Financing a construction contingency fund, which cannot exceed 10 percent of the total construction costs
- Paying professional fees directly attributable to the project such as architectural, legal and accounting fees.

Although loans under the certified development program are for communities and community agencies, individuals and small businesses benefit from such loans by applying through local development companies, discussed in Chapter 9.

SBA programs are subject to change not only as to requirements for participants but to the availability of funds, actions of Congress and the SBA Administrator, and the state of the economy. For updated information on current and existing loan programs, contact your nearest SBA office or their web site at www.sba.gov.

Which of the many sources of money for entrepreneurs will be the best for your depends on your needs and objectives. In the next chapter we'll talk about your attitudes about money, and offer some pointers on what you have to do to get financing.

Chapter **10**

Writing a Winning Loan Proposal

As we've pointed out in previous chapters, many people and organizations will invest in your business with you. They will provide the money and share the risks because; they are motivated by the desire to make more money.

Investors in small businesses hope to reap larger-than-normal rewards because of the higher-than-average risks. They realize they don't know or care enough about your particular business to make it successful without you, so they depend heavily on you to run the business well. In many ways, they feel as if they are investing in you, not just in your business. The quality of your ideas and your hard work makes you their equal. You need their money and they need your business.

In this chapter we will discuss how you actually get others involved financially. We'll help answer these questions:

- How much money will you need to start?
- How can you use a cash flow projection to build a loan proposal?
- What are the four steps in getting a loan?

At the end of this chapter is a sample loan proposal to review when developing your own.

STARTUP MONEY NEEDS

Without enough money to get you started and pay the bills until you show a profit, you will go broke. When this happens, a business is said to be undercapitalized. Being undercapitalized is one of the most common reasons a business fails. An undercapitalized business is really just an "underplanned" business.

That's why it's important to learn how to prepare, package and present a financing proposal for your business so that you can start with enough money to make it work profitably.

How much money will you need to start? The answer to this question is easy to understand, but hard to calculate. A new business needs enough money:

- to buy the equipment, tools, raw materials, inventory or whatever else it takes to build the products or provide the service it sells; and
- to pay the day-to-day operating expenses until the company shows a profit.

Most entrepreneurs are proud, resourceful people. They often feel uncomfortable asking for money; their initial tendency is to ask for too little. Being as optimistic as they are about the future of their enterprise, they assume that they can make everything work the way they want it to. As a result, many start their businesses with less money than they really need.

Vern's Painting Service

Vern's painting service is a sad but true case of poor planning. Vern thought he could get started on the money he planned to make from his first job. He bought some business cards and his first order of paint on credit, figuring that he could collect the money before the bills were due in 30 days. He didn't plan on having to buy an extra ladder, but, feeling pretty good about the amount of money he was making, he put it on his charge account with the paint supplier.

The job went reasonably well: Vern finished on time, even though he had to go back and get two more gallons of paint to get the right coverage. The customer paid him in full when he was finished, too. Unfortunately, on the way back from the job, his truck finally lost the exhaust pipe he had been patching together for the past few months. It took $187 to get it replaced, and that was $187 he didn't have. Since he wasn't working his regular job anymore, all of his regular expenses had to be picked up by his business in addition to the expenses for his first job. He was too tightly budgeted, and all it took was a bad bump on the road to throw him off.

In less than a month of business, Vern had already dug himself into a hole that looked deeper every day. He got so worried, he went back to his old job for the security of a regular paycheck. Because he wasn't out soliciting new customers and he wasn't available to answer the phone or make estimates, what little business he did have trickling in dried up almost immediately. By the third month, Vern was out of business, vowing never gain to do anything that crazy.

Judy's Web Site Design

Imagine another small business--this one a web site design service-that started with a good deal of planning up front. Judy thought carefully about where her customers were going to come from, how much they probably would spend with her each month and what kind of equipment she would need to service their needs. She took time to shop the market, get the right equipment to begin with and even approached a few of the customers to find out what kind of jobs they were interested in.

Judy was pleasantly surprised to find a few small companies that needed web sites created or maintained. She told customers she would handle the work at prearranged prices if they could assure her of the contract.

As a result of doing her homework, Judy was able to predict accurately what her monthly income was going to be. She felt confident about her figures for the first six months, and reasonably confident about the second six months. Based on these estimates, she was able to calculate her start-up costs and her operating expenses.

The moral of the story is simple: When Judy got the biggest projects of the year, as planned, she was ready for them. She had the cash she needed to pay an extra designer or content writer to work overtime on the jobs.

The difference between Vern and Judy is that one planned the financial side of the business, and the other didn't. One is still in business, and the other isn't.

THE IMPORTANCE FOR FINANCIAL PLANNING

You can do it right! There is nothing magical about financial planning, and it doesn't take a lot of formal training to do it. Basically, what you need to do is look ahead, imagine what is going to happen in your business, and then use your common sense!

Unfortunately, Vern's story is more typical than Judy's. Planning the finances is hard work, and not everyone likes to do it or realizes how important it is. Then, four or six or twelve months later, just as things are starting to roll, they find themselves out of money.

Instead of concentrating on delivering products and services to their customers, these entrepreneurs are running around town trying to arrange financing to pay their suppliers and the phone bill so they can stay in business. Since they can't take care of the customers at the same time, the customers get frustrated and begin to drift away. Sales and cash flow go down. As the situation gets more desperate, the small business owner runs faster and faster, trying to keep it all together. It becomes increasingly difficult to reverse the downward spiral; eventually, the businesses run out of time with the creditors and the entrepreneurs run out of energy and excuses. The poor management decisions lead to the initial undercapitalization, and the undercapitalization finally causes the business to fail.

CONSTRUCTING A CASH FLOW PROJECTION

Now we're going to look at an example of one and how it is used to build a loan proposal. A cash flow projection, sometimes called a pro forma, is a wonderful planning tool, because it can help you visualize the future. By imagining, or projecting, what you think you are going to sell and spend during the upcoming months, you can identify potential problems while there is still enough time to do something about them. Losing money on paper is a lot easier to take than losing real money, especially when it's your own!

By adding together all of the bottom lines, that is, the monthly profits or losses, you will be able to see your cumulative cash flow. Look at how the bottom line changes in the following example.

Frank's Delicatessen

Frank Stone, a manager for a local fast food franchise, decided to open a delicatessen. Frank did his homework well and developed a complete business plan for his deli.

Included in his business plan was a cash flow statement or projection for the period prior to his opening and for the first 12 month afterward. (see Figure 10.1)

In looking at the cash flow projection, we can see that Frank is going to need $49,175 before he opens his deli. This includes the following expenditures:

Purchases	$10,800
Salaries	4,500
Payroll Taxes	675
Capital Purchases	33,200
Total Expenditures	**$49,175**

What does this cash flow projection tell us about Frank's business? First, it tells us a lot about how he spends his money and is very helpful in determining how much he will need to run his business. Here is a list of the equipment Frank's company will need:

The cash flow projection also shows that Frank is planning to raise $54,167, as well as where he is going to get the money.

Mortgage	$25,000
Bank Loan	15,000
Owner's Cash	14,167
Total Receipts	**$54,167**

Therefore, deducting his pre-opening expenses of $49,175 from his total receipts, Frank will have $4,992 in cash prior to his opening.

Frank's Cash Flow Over Time What else can we learn from Frank's cash flow projections? We can see just when and how much income he will receive. Frank will start operating his deli with $4,992. After his first month, his cash will decline to $2,129; at the end of the second month, he will have only $1,451; and at the end of his fourth month, he will have $1,110. By the tenth month, however, Frank will have $6,687 in cash, exceeding the amount of cash he had when he opened the deli.

FIGURE 10.1- FRANK'S DELICATESSEN CASH FLOW STATEMENT

	Pre Start Up	Month 1	Month 2	Month 3	Month 4
Beginning Cash	0	4,992	2,159	1,451	1,268
Receipts					
Cash Sales		18,000	18,500	19,000	19,500
Mortgage	25,000				
Bank Loan	15,000				
Owner's Cash	14,167				
Total Receipts	54,167	18,000	18,500	19,000	19,500
Expenditures					
Purchases	10,800	8,000	8,225	8,450	8,675
Salaries	4,500	7,000	7,000	7,000	7,000
Payroll Taxes	675	1,050	1,050	1,050	1,050
Advertising		1,000	750	500	500
Dues		50			
Professional		500	50	50	50
Office Supplies		100	100	100	100
Telephone		100	100	100	100
Utilities		762	762	762	762
Miscellaneous		500	200	200	200
Insurance		500			250
Rent		300	300	300	300
Tax & License		300			
Interest-Loan		125	123	122	120
Interest-Mortgage		208	207	206	205
Loan Principal		201	203	204	206
Mortgage Principal		117	118	119	120
Capital Purchases	33,200				
Total Expenditures	49,175	20,833	19,208	19,183	19,658
Ending Cash	4,992	2,159	1,451	1,268	1,110

Month 5	Month 6	Month 7	Month 8	Month 9	Month 10	Month 11	Month 12
1,110	1,477	1,869	2,536	3,728	5,195	6,687	8,704
20,000	20,500	21,000	21,500	22,000	22,500	23,000	23,500
20,000	20,500	21,000	21,500	22,000	22,500	23,000	23,500
8,900	9,125	9,350	9,575	9,800	10,025	10,250	10,475
7,000	7,000	7,000	7,000	7,000	7,000	7,000	7,000
1,050	1,050	1,050	1,050	1,050	1,050	1,050	1,050
500	750	500	500	500	750	500	500
50	50	50	50	50	50	50	50
100	100	100	100	100	100	100	100
120	120	120	120	120	120	120	120
762	762	762	762	762	762	762	762
200	200	200	200	200	200	200	200
		250					
300	300	300	300	300	300	300	300
118	116	115	113	111	109	108	106
204	203	202	201	200	199	198	197
208	210	211	213	215	217	218	220
121	122	123	124	125	126	127	128
19,633	20,108	20,333	20,308	20,533	21,008	20,983	21,208
1,477	1,869	2,536	3,728	5,195	6,687	8,704	10,996

More than enough Instead of getting "just enough" to get started, Frank used a good rule of thumb he learned from his banker: H began his company with enough money to purchase his initial equipment and supplies ($49,175), plus the amount he thought he would need to cover his expenses in the early months, in addition to his deli sales.

Rather than getting "just enough" - which probably would have been just enough to get himself into trouble - he got enough money to succeed. He planned extra money for unexpected problems. Now, if he needs to make repairs on his equipment, or if the price of supplies goes up, or if business doesn't come in as planned, he will be able to ride out the situation and be around to profit another day.

You must do this for your business, too. Before you start looking for ways to cut corners or start operating on less than you should, find out how much it would realistically cost to run your business the right way. Multiply the lowest point in your cash flow by 150 percent or even 200 percent, and you will be very near the actual amount you will end up spending. This is the amount of money you need to get your business started. If you follow this rule and you have carefully thought through all of the expenses to include on your cash flow projections, you will not suffer from under capitalization.

BASIC FINANCIAL PRINCIPLES

Now we've come to one of the essential principles of small business, the basis of this book - finding ways of using other people's money to begin or continue your venture. The financial community calls this "sharing the pie". When you use other people's money, you are telling them that if they let you use their money in the beginning to get started or keep it going, you will share your profits with them later. That way, you both make more money. In economists' terms this the creation of wealth, and it's one of the fundamental components of our free enterprise system.

Getting someone else involved is a decision that you must think about carefully. The easiest or the cheapest source of money is not always the best. There may be strings or unreasonable conditions attached.

Three Stages in Financing a Business

There are basically three stages in financing a business: seed money, start-up financing and growth financing. These reflect the three basic stages in a business's life cycle.

Seed Money Seed money is used in the very earliest stages of a business. The amount of money needed here can be quite small. It is used to organize and plan the project. Joe and Doris used their personal money for this stage to drive around town talking to building owners about their contract plowing service. It cost them several hundred dollars in travel expenses, lost wages from Joe's regular job, lunches, letters, postage, letterhead and the like. A restaurant entrepreneur might use this time and money to make a site selection and have an architect do some preliminary drawings of the restaurant.

Start-up Financing This is the money it will take to get the doors open and get the business started. Joe and Doris need $11,250 for this stage.

Growth Financing Growth Financing is usually needed after a year or so of successful operation. Joe and Doris might want to buy some more new equipment or set up a similar type of operation in a nearby community once all the bugs worked out and they have turned the corner of their one-store operation. (By "turning the corner," the Smith's are showing consistent profits.) The restaurant entrepreneur might want to open another location or two, or even start franchising his idea if it turns out to be profitable.

PACKAGING YOUR IDEA

Once you have decided how much you need, you will be almost ready to start discussing your situation with people who can help you. First, you have to package your idea. In a way, you have to sell someone else on your dream; to persuade them to part with their cash, you have to convince them that you are worth the investment.

Where you get your money depends largely on how much you need. Different sources are comfortable with different amounts. Generally, the more money you want, the more packaging you need, and the more lengthy your written proposal.

Yes, you will have to write your proposal. For obvious reasons, this is still the best way to get your story in front of a lot of people quickly, professionally and in consistently. But don't despair if you aren't comfortable with writing; there are many people who can help you. The important part is your ideas; if you can't do it alone, find someone with whom to work. Look at it this way: Being able to meet this challenge is one of your first managerial tests!

Here's how you package or present your situation to a potential investor or lender:

FOUR STEPS TOWARD GETTING YOUR LOAN

STEP 1: Develop a Business Plan.

In the financial community, this is the basic tool you need. It is a report that tells the investor or lender that you have thoroughly planned your business. It is designed to give the lender confidence in you. If you don't need very much money, say $15,000 or less, you may not need to write a complicated plan, but you should at least have thought enough about each of the aspects of the business plan to be able to discuss them with an investor or lender.

Basically, the business plan answers the following questions in a logical order:

1. What is the business?
2. Which will be the most profitable products?
3. What are the major markets and competitors?

It also presents the budget and cash flow projections for at least the next 12 months.

In Lenore's case, she didn't feel he needed a business plan for her photography business. She was right; her $11,250 was a relatively small amount of money for straightforward needs. She did think about each of the components thoroughly, however, because she knew that some people would push her just enough to find out how much she really knew about her business.

STEP 2: Investigate Potential Sources of Capital

After you have done your basic planning and have prepared your loan proposal of up to 10 pages, you can start looking for the best source for the amount of money you need. Lenore's photography business needed $11,250; this is a lot of money to some people, and not enough for others to bother with. Because the $11,250 was not a large amount of money, Lenore had several possible sources for the money, including her brother, who had previously offered to loan her money, and two friends, one of whom was her hairdresser.

STEP 3: Prepare a Loan Proposal

This is required for all but the most informal financing arrangements. It is like a mini-business plan, about 10 pages in length, and is tailored specifically to a single investor or lender. Because it is short, each one can be customized to show each prospective lender or investor the information that is needed or requested. This becomes the "talking tool" in your negotiations for money and includes the following information:

- A brief summary of your business, including what your business is, what products you sell and the general types of competition you have.

- A brief history of yourself and your business to date, including any other financing.

- An explanation of the proposal: what amount of money you need, what terms are preferred, repayment preference, collateral available, equity options available and any other information that is relevant to your specific request for funds.

- Appropriate financial statements: balance sheet, earnings history (if any) and financial projections for three years.

- Credit, personal and business references.

Lenore put together a very successful financing proposal for his business. It did its job; it got her the money she needed on terms that made sense for her. Later in this chapter, we will take a close look at a typical loan proposal so you can see exactly how to put yours together.

STEP 4: Present Your Materials to Your Prospective Lenders or Investors.

This can be a formal presentation or an informal discussion, depending upon whom you are meeting with. One of the people who expressed interest in Lenore's business turned out to be her hairdresser; she was interested in investing the whole $11,250.

When Lenore made her presentation, she did it over coffee at a restaurant near the hair salon. Later, she made a much more formal presentation to a loan officer at a bank downtown.

That's all there is to it: 1-2-3-4, and you've got the money you need to start and run your business. You can do this, too; hundreds of thousands of people are getting millions of dollars to start and run their dreams every year.

For the rest of this chapter, we will concentrate on filling in the rest of the "hows" related to getting money, such as:

- How do you find people who are able to lend money or invest?
- How do you approach them and ask them if they are interested in your proposition?
- How do you make a successful presentation?

By the time you have finished this chapter, you will be fully prepared to get the money you need. You will be able to hold your own in conversations with other businesspeople, investors and lenders. In short, you will have learned what it takes to put money behind your dreams. Rather than just being a bystander, you can be an active contender.

HOW TO PUT YOUR LOAN PROPOSAL TOGETHER

No matter which source of money you approach, you will need to sell them on your concept. As we discussed before, a loan proposal is the best tool to use in telling your story. This is true even if you plan to use a more complete business plan.

Your loan proposal is such a common document in the marketplace and is so important to your success that you must make the commitment it takes to settle down and write it. No part of your loan proposal takes more than a page or two; if you break it into bite-sized pieces, you should be able to put it into a rough draft stage after only a few evenings' work.

Your proposal must fit your needs, wants and background. It must also fit the needs and interests of the investor or lender to whom you are applying for financing.

Figure 10.2 Loan Proposal Outline

- Cover Page: Loan Proposal to name of bank, from whom, and date Loan amount and use of funds
- Description of the business (or proposed business)
- Specific use of funds
- Catalog pages, literature, quotations supporting the use of the funds, how funds will be spent
- Projected Income Statement for the business covering one year
- Projected Balance Sheet for the business after one year
- Source of funds to be invested in business in addition to the proposed bank loan
- Personal financial statement of owners
- List of credit references
- List of present and past business associates
- Personal background of applicant
- How and when loan is to be repaid

Be brief and to the point in your proposal. Most will probably spend only five to ten minutes reviewing it. If your key points and plans are not immediately evident and clearly presented, keep working at it until it is tight and well-written.

Here are some simple guidelines to keep in mind as you begin writing:

- Say it straight. Your loan proposal should be realistic and honest. Anticipate any negative reactions and address them squarely.
- Match each proposal page to suit your reader. If you are asking for a loan from one group and an equity investment from another, parts of the proposal

will change for each.
- Write in a smooth, comfortable style.
- Don't rush and don't write when you are too tired to think clearly.
- Don't overstate figures or purposes.
- Follow the outline as shown in Figure 10.2
- Your loan proposal must by typed for a professional look.

Using Joe and Doris's company Smith's Snow Plowing, Lawn Care and Landscape Services as a model, we have developed a complete example of a bank loan proposal which appears in Figure 10.3, at the end of this chapter.

All you have to do to develop your own loan proposal is to substitute your name, business, money needs, etc. in each applicable page as you prepare your own.

ASKING FOR YOUR LOAN

Now that Joe and Doris have completed their loan proposal, they are ready to meet with their banker.

Eight years before they even considered having a business of their own, they did one other very important thing: They opened a joint checking account at the local branch office of the First Bank of Anywhere.

Over the past eight years, they took out two small loans from the bank. The first was to finance an automobile purchase three years ago. Then, last year, they took out a $5,000 loan to remodel their kitchen and breezeway. While doing this, they became well acquainted with Ted Benson, the bank's vice president for commercial lending.

When they first considered going into their snow plowing and lawn care service, they casually mentioned to Mr. Benson that they might see him for a business loan. Thus, they had paved the way to set an appointment with their bank for a business loan.

If your banking experience has been limited, consider taking all or some of the following steps:

- Open a personal checking account with a commercial bank.
- Ask to meet a bank officer when you open your account. Even the president is not too high on the ladder. If he or she is not available, ask to meet a vide president.
- Ask to see this same person from time to time when you come into the bank to make a deposit or to cash a check. Simply go over and say "hello".
- If you already have a checking account open, consider opening a savings account.
- Take out a loan, even if it is a small one, to establish a loan history with your bank.

In short, establish a personal relationship with a specific individual at your bank. This relationship is best developed over a period of time. Otherwise, when you do ask for a loan, you simply have to meet with a loan officer.

Then, when your plans are in place, make an appointments to discuss your loan and state that you wish to present you loan proposal. Do not discuss the proposal at this time.

At the meeting, present you loan proposal to the bank officer. He or she will probably ask you some questions and indicate if your loan request will need to be presented to a loan committee. If you have a loan history with the bank, you may hear within a few days. Naturally, the higher the amount of the loan request, the greater the number of questions you may be asked.

Loan Proposal to

FIRST NATIONAL BANK OF ANYWHERE

from

**SMITH' SNOW PLOWING, LAWN CARE
And LANDSCAPE SERVICES**

September 10, 200X

TABLE OF CONTENTS

May 1, 20XX
Example Loan Proposal
(Page 1)

LOAN AMOUNT AND USE OF FUNDS

Joe and Doris Smith, owners and operators of SMITH'S SNOW PLOWING, LAWN CARE AND LANDSCAPING SERVICES, INC. apply for a loan from the FIRST NATIONAL BANK in the amount of $35,000. This money will be used as follows:

Working Capital-Payroll	$7,000
Truck	18,000
Lawn Mower Purchases	3,500
Snow Plow Attachment	3,000
Computer & Software	3,500
Total	$35,000

SMITH'S SNOW PLOWING, LAWN CARE AND
LANDSCAPING SERVICES

SMITH'S SNOW PLOWING, LAWN CARE AND LANDSCAPING SERVICES, INC. is being formed by Joe and Doris Smith. The Company will provide snow plowing, lawn cutting and landscaping services during the appropriate seasons of the year. These services will be offered to homeowners and commercial customers.

The Company plans to rent 4,000 square feet of office and warehouse space at Industrial Park, located at 3500 East Superior Boulevard. Immediately adjacent to the building is a two-acre site, zoned agricultural, which the Smith's purchased two years ago. This site has a well on it and will be used to maintain an inventory of trees, shrubs and other landscape materials.

For the past two years, Joe Smith has run a part-time landscape business, which he operated as a sole proprietor under the name of Joe Smith Landscaping. The business has been very successful. During these two years, he had a net profit of $6,500 for the first year and $14,000 for the second year. He has operated primarily in the western suburbs, which is the part of the city having the fastest growth in home building and commercial development. Projections and statistics furnished by the city planning department indicate that this growth will continue.

Recognizing this fact, and that Joe has had such good success running a part-time landscaping business, both he and Doris feel they could be very successful by expanding into a full-time landscaping business together with lawn cutting and snow plowing services.

They have canvassed the neighborhood extensively, talking with past landscape customers and prospects. They have already signed contracts with 42 homeowners to provide lawn care services. Thirty of these homeowners have stated they would sign up

110

for their snow plowing services. In addition, they have verbal commitments for snow removal at the parking lots of four companies.

Joe and Doris Smith incorporated under the laws of the State of Minnesota.

SPECIFIC USE OF LOAN FUNDS

Payroll		$5,000
Insurance		500
Office Supplies	300	
Gasoline	500	
Tools	<u>400</u>	
Business Supplies		<u>1,200</u>
Total Working Capital		$6,700
Used 4-Wheel Drive Ford Pickup Truck		
with Snow Plow Attachment		$20,600
Lawn Mower Purchases		
2-Toro Riding Mowers, Commercial	2,300	
1-Toro 21-inch self-propelled	1,000	
Other Toro Accessories	<u>1,000</u>	
Total Mowers		4,300
Office Supplies		
Computer, Software & Supplies	950	
Printer	450	
2-Used Office Desks	800	
2-Office Chairs	500	
2-4-drawer Filing Cabinets	200	
Office Supplies	<u>500</u>	
Total Office Supplies		<u>3,400</u>
Total Funds Needed		**$35,000**

Example Loan Proposal

(Page 4)

ED SUNDEEN LAWN EQUIPMENT SALES
127 Queens Blvd

Minneapolis, MN 55499

612-555-0000 Fax 612-555-1111

April 29, 20XX

SMITH'S SNOW PLOWING AND LAWN CARE SERVICES

Joe Smith

1423 Pender Road

Anywhere, USA 12345

QUOTATION NUMBER 7589

2 Toro Riding Mowers, Commercial 11 HP Model 30111	$2,300
2 Toro 21-Inch Self-Propelled Mowers	1,000
Toro Accessories	1,000
Total	$4,300

This quotation is good for 60 days from date of quotation.

All prices delivered FOB Minneapolis, Dealer showroom.

Thank You

Ed Sundeen

Owner, Manager

113

**SMITH'S SNOW PLOWING, LAWN CARE
AND LANDSCAPE SERVICES, INC.
PROJECTED INCOME STATEMENT
FOR THE FIRST YEAR ENDED DECEMBER 31, 20XX**

SALES

Lawn Services	$60,000	
Landscaping Services	30,000	
Snow Plowing	40,000	
Total Sales		$150,000
COST OF SALES (Trees etc)		32,000
GROSS PROFIT		$118,000

**OPERATING
EXPENSES**

Salaries	50,000	
Payroll Taxes	10,000	
Rent	5,000	
Advertising	2,100	
Insurance	2,500	
Car/Truck Expenses	5,000	
Telecommunications	900	
Office Supplies	2,900	
Repair/Maintenance	3,000	
Miscellaneous	1,500	
Depreciation	5,500	
Interest	2,850	
Total Operating Expenses		$91,250
Income before Taxes		$26,750

**SMITH'S SNOW PLOWING, LAWN CARE
AND LANDSCAPE SERVICES, INC.
PROJECTED INCOME STATEMENT
FOR THE SECOND YEAR ENDED DECEMBER 31, 20X1**

SALES

Lawn Services	$50,000	
Landscaping Services	40,000	
Snow Plowing	120,000	
Total Sales		$210,000
COST OF SALES (Trees etc)		40,000
GROSS PROFIT		$170,000

OPERATING EXPENSES

Salaries	80,000	
Payroll Taxes	16,000	
Rent	6,000	
Advertising	4,000	
Insurance	3,000	
Car/Truck Expenses	8,000	
Telecommunications	1,200	
Office Supplies	3,900	
Repair/Maintenance	5,000	
Miscellaneous	2,500	
Depreciation	5,500	
Interest	2,000	
Total Operating Expenses		$137,100

Income before Taxes $32,900

SMITH'S SNOW PLOWING, LAWN CARE
AND LANDSCAPE SERVICES, INC.
PROJECTED BALANCE SHEETS
AS OF DECEMBER 31

ASSETS

	YEAR 1	YEAR 2
Current Assets		
Cash	$6,500	$17,600
Accounts Receivable	15,300	14,000
Inventories	3,500	16,000
Total Current Assets	25,300	47,600
Fixed Assets		
Land	12,000	12,000
Truck	18,000	18,000
Snow Plow Attachment	3,000	3,000
Lawn Care Equipment	3,500	3,500
Landscape Equipment	9,500	9,500
Office Equipment	5,500	5,500
Less Accum Depreciation	(7,725)	(18,025)
Total Fixed Assets	43,775	33,475
Total Assets	$69,075	$81,075

LIABILITIES & STOCKHOLDERS' EQUITY

	YEAR 1	YEAR 2
Current Liabilities		
Accounts Payable	$6,000	$19,000
Bank Loan	35,000	24,000
Total Liabilities	41,000	43,000
Owner's Equity	28,075	38,075
Total Liabilities & Owner's Equity	$69,075	$81,075

116

SOURCE OF FUNDS TO BE INVESTED
IN BUSINESS IN ADDITION TO THE BANK LOAN

Mr. and Mrs. Joseph Smith	$4,500
From Savings Bank	500
Equipment & Machinery from Joe Smith Landscaping	9,500
Two-Acre Land Site, Valued at Cost	12,000
Total	$26,500

The two-acre tract of land adjacent to the building that Smith's Snow Plowing, Lawn Care and Landscape Services, Inc. will use was purchased two years ago by Doris and Joseph Smith for cash.

Example Loan Proposal
(Page 9)

NOTE: This section is to attach the bank's standard application form. It will have a section for
your personal assets and liabilities.

CREDIT REFERENCES

First National Bank, 444 S. Fourth St., Anywhere

National Oil Co., P.O. Box 1111, New Amsterdam, NY 10001

Onion Oil Co., 99 Cooper Lane, Grover, OH 54622

Mesa Department Store, 8th at Love Streets, Anywhere

MacAdams Jewelers, 1234 Pine St., Anywhere

American Express Co., P.O. Box 1984, Old York, NY 10001

Shoppers Charge, P.O. Box 1234, Jaxon, TX 76357

PERSONAL REFERENCES

Rev. James Bardy, 9674 Waverly St., Anywhere 555-6262

Samuel Bloom, MD, 4646 Cotton St., Anywhere 555-9273

Robert Krasner, DDS, 1212 South St., Anywhere 555-3546

Mr. Robert Joyce, 7777 Vegas Lane, Reno, IL 312-555-7777

Mrs. Erica Sloan, 2035 No 47th Place, Anywhere 555-9999

PRESENT AND PAST BUSINESS ASSOCIATES

Mr. T.S. Gardner, Trivial Motors, 22 South St., Anywhere 555-3544

Mr. J.R. Williams, President, Acme Electronics Co., Jackson, NE   33325 333-555-6668

Mrs. Shirley Welsome, Manager, Welsome Parts Store, 2nd at   South Streets, Anywhere 555-2222

Meyer Lobotsky, Manager, Van's Storage and Transfer, 4900 Branch Ave., Anywhere 555-8932

PERSONAL BACKGROUND
JOE & DORIS SMITH

Joe's first job was a groundskeeper for the Golden Valley Golf and Country Club, where he participated in golf course turf management and landscaping. After graduating from college, Joe worked for five years for the U.S. Department of Commerce in their field office, doing statistical work.

Joe then went with the Marketing Department of Jones Construction Company and worked in the area of Sales Promotion for six years. He also participated in bid preparations. After six years with the company, Joe took his current job with Trivial Motors, where he has worked for the past three years.

Two years ago, Joe started a part-time landscaping business under the name of Smith's Landscape Services.

Doris is with the Eagle Hills School District where she teaches the third grade in the Eagle Hill Elementary School. She has been with Eagle Hills for the past nine years.

In the first year of Smith's Landscape Services, Joe had sales of $18,000 and last year, had sales of $32,000. We have reinvested all of the earnings in the landscape equipment. We intend to use our business, sales and organizational skills to develop our newly expanded business. Doris will assist full-time during her summer break.

We have two children, a daughter, Emily, age 3; and a son, Adam, age 6.

Example Loan Proposal

(Page 12)

How Loan Is To Be Repaid

Joe and Doris Smith request that their loan of $35,000 be repaid as follows:

PRINCIPAL   Beginning August 1, 20XX their Business Checking Account will be charged $1,000 a month for the next 36 months until the loan is paid.

INTEREST   Beginning on the 1st day of each month following the beginning of the loan that the interest for the preceding period be charged against their business checking account.

It is understood that the interest will be on the unpaid balance of the loan.

Chapter **11**

How to Present Your Plan

All your documents are in shape, you've decided on the right bank and are dealing with the right loan officer. Now is the time to set up a presentation.

Generally, you will be making your presentation one-on-one to a lending officer, proving to him or her that you are credit worthy and the bank's money will be safe with you, thus enlisting his or her support of your loan application when it arrives at the bank's loan committee.

Sometimes, however, you will have to present your loan proposal to a group of investors. This chapter will show you how to make effective presentations to these larger audiences.

FOUR STEPS TO EFFECTIVE PRESENTATIONS

Presenting spoken information is different from writing it. An effective presentation includes four items: the opening, the preview, the major points, and the closing.

Opening

In speaking, your opening is even more important than in writing. You must immediately capture your listeners' interest while you establish your qualifications.

An attention-grabbing opening stimulates your listeners' curiosity so they will look forward to what you'll tell them in the course of your presentation. A good opening could include an interesting sidelight about your business or yourself, an important statistic or a pertinent story.

Preview

The preview is useful because listeners, unlike readers, cannot skim over the general outline of your presentation. Your preview will tell them, in general terms, just what they can expect to learn or what you want them to do as a result of your presentation. List your three to five main points; listeners always remember better if they hear an overview at the beginning of your talk.

Major Points

In the main part of your presentation it's important to make your major points clearly. Don't expect your audience to know as much as you do about the subject you're covering. Limit your main points, emphasize when you are changing to a new subject and repeat your important points. Listeners cannot accept as much information as readers can and do not usually remember information they hear only once.

Closing

Your audience is probably going to remember your last statements. For your closing, avoid saying things like, "Well, that's about it," or "That's all I have to say." Move into your closing with a strong phrase such as "to summarize" or "in conclusion," and then restate your major points to reinforce the message.

VISUAL AIDS

Most people speak at about 100 words a minute, but can understand 400 to 1,000 words per minute. No matter how terrific you may be at presenting information, It's easy for the audience's attention to drift. A good way to keep listeners involved is to give them something visual to keep them concentrating on your ideas.

Visual aids range in type from printed materials to flip charts, to a full computer visual presentation. Decide which best meets your needs, based on the situation and your personal preferences. You can always combine various kinds of visual aids when they're called for.

In some situations you'll be limited to the simplest props; an agenda at the beginning of your presentation or a printed handout at the end. One excellent technique for involving an audience is to write down points as you make them; on a blank flipchart or overhead transparency. Use this method only if you feel comfortable with it. Nothing is worse than giving your listeners the sense that you are not fully in control of your information or materials.

Another way to use flip charts or overhead transparencies is to have them prepared with an outline of your information that you can point to during the presentation. As an added twist, you can leave blanks to fill in at the appropriate time or to even cross out some items and write over them to make your points more dramatically.

The most professional visual aids are those you create and package before the presentation. Professionally prepared flip charts, wall cards, charts, or computer graphic shows provide excellent support for a smooth performance.

Tips for Using Graphics

Once you have decided on the techniques to use you are ready to create your aids. Here are some rules you should follow to gain the most effectiveness:

- Use visual aids only if they explain your points better than you could by just speaking them. Remember, you're the star; your visual aids are the supporting players.
- Keep it simple. Trim your notes to key words and phrases. Don't write complete sentences. Reduce graphs to a minimum of detail.
- Keep it easy to read. Use large, clear, bold, well-spaced lettering and graphs. Don't include more than ten lines per page or slide.
- If you use colors to brighten and help clarify your message, be consistent. For example, use one color for major points and another for minor items or one color for ideas and another for financial matters. Dark blues, blacks, reds, and greens are best for type and graphs. Yellows and oranges are good for backgrounds. Save your darkest, highest contrast color for your most important point.
- Make each slide or page a completely self contained unit.
- Always provide a heading.
- Avoid passive statements, use the active voice always:
  Not: "The financial review should be issued by May 1."
  Better: "Review performance of all departments will be ready by May 1."
- Emphasize main ideas, do not bury them.
- Group similar ideas together.
- The best way to demonstrate relationships clearly is with a chart or graphs

FINAL PREPARATIONS

Even expert public speakers need memory aids to ensure that they cover all points. The best method is to copy an outline of your talk to 5 x 7 or 4 x 6 cards. These cards are easy to hold and allow you to add, subtract or rearrange your material easily. These cards are to be used for notes only. Do not write your presentation on them word-for-word; that would make you a reader, not a speaker. Each card should contain about five minutes' worth of material, printed large enough for you to see easily.

Once you have organized your presentation and prepared any visual aids you may need, it's time to practice your presentation. Practice will help you increase your self-confidence and improve your wording, identify any flaws in your speech and make sure your visual aids work smoothly with the content of your presentation.

Rehearse out loud, standing up, and use your visual aids just as you will in the actual presentation. It might help to rehearse in front of a mirror or record it on an audiotape or videotape so you can review your performance. Give your talk to a friend and get his or her suggestions. At this point, you want to improve your vocal expression and enthusiasm, and make your delivery as clear as possible.

The object is not to memorize the exact words or read your speech. It is a good idea, however, to memorize the opening and closing of your presentation. This will help you establish eye contact with your audience members when it's most crucial to gain their interest, support and approval.

Most important, keep cool. If you know your material and you've done your homework you should be ready for any audience. Be confident. Winston Churchill, one of the world's great speakers, said that when he felt anxious before a speech he would stop for a moment and reassured himself with the thought, "Look at those cabbage heads. They're just people, I have nothing to fear from them."

Chapter 12

The Bottom Line

P. T. Barnum, who certainly knew how to make money, said it over a century ago: "Money is a terrible master but an excellent servant." Truly these are words to borrow by. With this in mind, let's review the 11 guidelines for finding money for your small business.

ELEVEN GUIDELINES FOR FINDING MONEY FOR YOUR SMALL BUSINESS

1. Money is simply a tool that helps your business reach its goals. Not borrowing money when you need it is as bad as borrowing too much money that you can't repay.
2. By asking for a loan, you are really asking a lender to be your business partner.
3. Lenders are in business of making loans.
4. Lenders will only lend money they expect will be paid back and be profitable for them.
5. It's your responsibility to convince the lender that your business can and will pay back its loan.
6. Financial planning is basically about using your common sense in forecasting what is going to happen in your business.
7. Too many entrepreneurs start or operate their business with less money than they will really need.
8. Cash Flow or pro forma projections can help you see problems coming while there is still enough time to do something about them.
9. Writing a business plan forces you to think enough about every aspect of

how the business is to operate to be able to discuss them with an investor or lender.

10. Establishing an ongoing business relationship is just as important as getting financing. You never know when you'll have to go back to the well for more money.

11. Every loan application is a new beginning.

Money Is a Tool

Money means a lot of different things to people, but the only way a serious businessperson can make the most of money is to understand that it is simply a tool that helps your business reach its goals. Not borrowing money when you need it, and can repay it, is as bad as borrowing too much money that can't be repaid.

You're Really Looking For a Partner

When you approach a lender you are asking him or her to be your business partner. The money he or she lends you is an investment in your ideas, your business ability and your dependability as a person.

Lending Money Is the Lender's Business

Remember, lenders are in the business of making loans, and they are always out to make the best loan record they can. They will only lend money they anticipate will be paid back and be profitable for them. Unlike family members or friends, their interest is strictly business, so they have to be careful about the people and companies to whom they lend money and how they do it. Remember, a bank must make 97 good loans to make up for one bad loan.

You Must Sell the Lender on Your Business

It's your responsibility to convince the lender that your business is one that can and will pay back its loan. Before you go looking for a loan, make sure that you have done all the planning and preparation. A good loan proposal must persuade a lender that it is in his or her interest to lend you money.

You will have to show the lender how the business is going to repay the loan. To do that, you have to prepare a financial plan as evidence that you know what you are doing and how you are preparing for success. You have to demonstrate that you've thought through as many of the business problems that you can foresee. In a way, you have to sell others on your dream - and in order to persuade them to part with their cash, you have to convince them that you are worth the investment.

128

Make Sure Your Company is Adequately Capitalized

A new or established business needs enough money to:

- Buy the equipment, tools, raw materials, inventory or whatever else it takes to build the products or provide the service it sells; and

- Pay the day-to-day operating expenses until the profits begin or are large enough to cover all expenses.

Most businesses that fail, do so because they were undercapitalized; they didn't have, or were unable to get, enough money to pay their bills. In most cases this occurs due to poor planning. Too many entrepreneurs start their businesses, or work day to day, with less money than they really need, assuming everything will work out the way they want it to. And when their company hits a rough spot, this poor planning can lead to an unnecessary business failure.

Doing It Right: The Four Basic Steps

Financial planning is basically about looking ahead and forecasting what is going to happen in your business, and then using your common sense! There are four basic steps you must take in preparing a financial plan: prepare a cash flow projection, a business plan and a loan proposal, and then explore potential sources of capital.

The Cash Flow Projection. In previous chapters, we discussed what goes into a cash flow or pro forma projection. This excellent planning tool can help you visualize the future. By projecting what you think you are going to sell and spend during the upcoming months, you can foresee problems coming while there is still enough time to do something about them.

The Business Plan Basically, the business plan answers the following questions:

1. What is the business?
2. Which will be the most profitable products?
3. What are the major markets and competitors?

It also presents the budget and cash flow projections for at least the next 12 months.

Writing a business plan forces you to think enough about each of the aspects of how the business is to operate, so that you can discuss them with an investor or lender. The business plan is important because it tells the investor or lender that you have thoroughly charted your business. It is designed to give them confidence in you.

The Loan Proposal The loan proposal is required for all but the most informal financing arrangements. It offers the best way to get your story out to a lot of people quickly and professionally as you shop for money. Think of your loan proposal as a mini-business plan that can easily be customized to show each prospective lender or investor the information that is needed or requested.

Your proposal must fit your needs, wants and background. It must also fit the needs and interests of the investor or lender to whom you are applying for financing.

Potential Sources of Capital After you have done your basic planning and have prepared your loan proposal, you can start looking for the best source for the amount of money you need.

Where you get your money is largely dependent upon how much you need. Various sources are comfortable with different amounts. Generally, the more money you want, the more "packaging" you need and the more lengthy your written proposal.

Have a Realistic Attitude

Remember, the golden rule in business is, he or she who has the gold makes the rules. If you go into the money market with unrealistic attitudes about money and the people who lend it, you're in for some disappointments and frustration. The only practical way to obtain financing is to view the process objectively. This is a business arrangement, pure and simple.

Invest in Your Own Idea

Lenders want to see if you believe in your company enough to risk all or part of your personal assets. They could decide that if you don't have enough confidence to guarantee the debt, you should not be borrowing the money.

Don't Burn Your Bridges

Getting financing is important, but establishing an ongoing business relationship is just as important. You never know when you'll have to go back to the well for more money. Being truthful with the lender, repaying your loans and fulfilling all your commitments will help to establish your business credit rating not only with your initial lender but for any financial dealings you'll have in the years to come.

Every Loan Application Is A New Beginning

A loan refusal is only one lender's judgment of the uncertainty involved in that loan request. It is not an evaluation of your worth as a person.

Even if your first plan doesn't pan out, you'll soon get better at forecasting with experience. Every newly approached lender gives you a fresh opportunity to make your case better. Learn the lessons or your previous rejections and determine not to repeat them.

Money Is the Key to Success in Business

Our hope and intention, with this book, is to give you the necessary information and background to make finding money sources and getting funding for your ideas as painless as possible. As with everything else in life, the better you follow the lessons of the practices we've presented and prepare for your day with the lenders the more successful you will be.

APPENDIX A

Small Business Administration Forms

Application for Business Loan	Form 4
SBA LowDoc Application	Form 4
Personal Financial Statement	Form 413
Application for Small Business Loan (Short Form)	Form 4
Schedule of Collateral	Exhibit A
Statement of Personal History	Form 912

U.S. Small Business Administration

APPLICATION FOR BUSINESS LOAN

OMB Approval No: 3245-0016
Expiration Date: 11/30/04

Individual	Full Address	

Name of Applicant Business	Tax I.D. No. or SSN

Full Street Address of Business	Tel. No. (inc. A/C)

City	County	State	Zip	Number of Employees (Including subsidiaries and affiliates)
Type of Business		Date Business Established		At Time of Application _____
Bank of Business Account and Address				If Loan is Approved _____
				Subsidiaries or Affiliates (Separate for above) _____

Use of Proceeds: (Enter Gross Dollar Amounts Rounded to the Nearest Hundreds)	Loan Requested		Loan Request
Land Acquisition		Payoff SBA Loan	
New Construction/ Expansion Repair		Payoff Bank Loan (Non SBA Associated	
Acquisition and/or Repair of Machinery and Equipment		Other Debt Payment (Non SBA Associated)	
Inventory Purchase		All Other	
Working Capital (including Accounts Payable)		Total Loan Requested	
Acquisition of Existing Business		Term of Loan - (Requested Mat.)	_____ Yrs.

PREVIOUS SBA OR OTHER FEDERAL GOVERNMENT DEBT: If you or any principals or affiliates have 1) ever requested Government Financing or 2) are delinquent on the repayment of any Federal Debt complete the following:

Name of Agency	Original Amount of Loan	Date of Request	Approved or Declined	Balance	Current or Past Due
	$			$	
	$			$	

ASSISTANCE List the name(s) and occupation of anyone who assisted in the preparation of this form, other than applicant.

Name and Occupation	Address	Total Fees Paid	Fees Due
Name and Occupation	Address	Total Fees Paid	Fees Due

Note: The estimated burden completing this form is 12.0 hours per response. You will not be required to respond to any collection of information unless it displays a currently valid OMB approval number. Comments on the burden should be sent to U.S. Small Business Administration, Chief, AIB, 409 3rd St., S.W., Washington, D.C. 20416 and Desk Office for Small Business Administration, Office of Management and Budget, New Executive Office Building, room 10202 Washington, D.C. 20503. OMB Approval (3245-0016). **PLEASE DO NOT SEND FORMS TO OMB.**
SUBMIT COMPLETED APPLICATION TO LENDER OF CHOICE

SBA Form 4 (8-01) Use Previous Edition Until Exhausted

Federal Recycling Program   Printed on Recycled Paper

Page 1

This form was electronically produced by Elite Federal Forms, Inc.

ALL EXHIBITS MUST BE SIGNED AND DATED BY PERSON SIGNING THIS FORM

BUSINESS INDEBTEDNESS: Furnish the following information on all installment debts, contracts, notes, and mortgages payable. Indicate by an asterisk (*) items to be paid by loan proceeds and reason for paying them (present balance should agree with the latest balance sheet submitted).

To Whom Payable	Original Amount	Original Date	Present Balance	Rate of Interest	Maturity Date	Monthly Payment	Security	Current or Past Due
Acct. #	$		$			$		
Acct. #	$		$			$		
Acct. #	$		$			$		
Acct. #	$		$			$		
Acct. #	$		$			$		

MANAGEMENT (Proprietor, partners, officers, directors, all holders of outstanding stock – <u>100% of ownership must be shown</u>). Use separate sheet if necessary.

Name and Social Security Number and Position Title	Complete Address	%Owned	*Military Service From To		*Sex
Race*: American Indian/Alaska Native ☐ Black/African-Amer. ☐ Asian ☐ Native Hawaiian/Pacific Islander ☐ White ☐			**Ethnicity*** Hisp./Latino ☐ Not Hisp./Latino ☐		
Race*: American Indian/Alaska Native ☐ Black/African-Amer. ☐ Asian ☐ Native Hawaiian/Pacific Islander ☐ White ☐			**Ethnicity*** Hisp./Latino ☐ Not Hisp./Latino ☐		
Race*: American Indian/Alaska Native ☐ Black/African-Amer. ☐ Asian ☐ Native Hawaiian/Pacific Islander ☐ White ☐			**Ethnicity*** Hisp./Latino ☐ Not Hisp./Latino ☐		
Race*: American Indian/Alaska Native ☐ Black/African-Amer. ☐ Asian ☐ Native Hawaiian/Pacific Islander ☐ White ☐			**Ethnicity*** Hisp./Latino ☐ Not Hisp./Latino ☐		

*This data is collected for statistical purpose only. It has no bearing on the credit decision to approve or decline this application. One or more boxes may be selected.

THE FOLLOWING EXHIBITS MUST BE COMPLETED WHERE APPLICABLE. ALL QUESTIONS ANSWERED ARE MADE A PART OF THE APPLICATION.

For Guarantee Loans please provide an original and one copy (Photocopy is Acceptable) of the Application Form, and all Exhibits to the participating lender. For Direct Loans submit one original copy of the application and Exhibits to SBA.

1. Submit SBA Form 912 (Statement of Personal History) for each type of individual that the Form 912 requires.

2. If your collateral consists of (A) Land and Building, (B) Machinery and Equipment, (C) Furniture and Fixtures, (D) Accounts *Receivable*, (E) Inventory, (F) Other, please provide an itemized list (labeled Exhibit A) that contains serial and identification numbers for all articles that had an Original value of greater than $500. Include a legal description of Real Estate Offered as collateral.

3. Furnish a signed current personal balance sheet (SBA Form 413 may be used for this purpose) for each stockholder (with 20% or greater ownership), partner, officer, and owner. Include the assets and liabilities of the spouse and any close relatives living in the household. Also, include your Social Security Number. The date should be the same as the most recent business financial statement. Label it Exhibit B.

4. Include the financial statements listed below: a,b,c for the last three years; also a,b,c, and d as of the same date, - current within 90 days of filing the application; and statement e, if applicable. Label it Exhibit C (Contact SBA for referral if assistance with preparation is wanted.) **All** information must be <u>signed and dated</u>.

a. Balance Sheet
b. Profit and Loss Statement (if not available, explain why and substitute Federal income tax forms)
c. Reconciliation of Net Worth
d. Aging of Accounts Receivable and Payable (summary not
e. detailed)
   Projection of earnings for at least one year where financial statements for the last three years are unavailable or when SBA requests them.

5. Provide a brief history of your company and a paragraph describing the expected benefits it will receive from the loan. Label it Exhibit D.

6. Provide a brief description similar to a resume of the education, technical and business background for all the people listed under Management. Label it Exhibit E.

7. Submit the names, addresses, tax I.D. number(EIN or SSN), and current personal balance sheet(s) of any co-signers and/or guarantors for the loan who are not otherwise affiliated with the business as Exhibit F.

8. Include a list of any machinery or equipment or other non-real estate assets to be purchased with loan proceeds and the cost of each item as quoted by the seller as Exhibit G. Include the seller's name and address.

9. Have you or any officers of your company ever been involved in bankruptcy or insolvency proceedings? If so, please provide the details as Exhibit H. If none, check here:
    Yes   No

10. Are you or your business involved in any pending lawsuits? If yes, provide the details as Exhibit I.
If none, check here: Yes [No

11. Do you or your spouse or any member of your household, or anyone who owns, manages or directs your business or their spouses or members of their households work for the Small Business Administration, Small Business Advisory Council, SCORE or ACE, any Federal Agency, or the participating lender? If so, please provide the name and address of the person and the office where employed. Label this Exhibit J.
If none, check here:

12. Does your business, its owners or majority stockholders own or have a controlling interest in other businesses? If yes, please provide their names and the relationship with your company along with a current balance sheet and operating statement for each. This should be Exhibit K.

13. Do you buy from, sell to, or use the services of any concern in which someone in your company has a significant financial interest? If yes, provide details on a separate sheet of paper labeled Exhibit L.

14. If your business is a franchise, include a copy of the franchise agreement and a copy of the FTC disclosure statement supplied to you by the Franchisor. Please include it as Exhibit M.

CONSTRUCTION LOANS ONLY

15. Include as a separate exhibit (Exhibit N) the estimated cost of the project and a statement of the source of any additional funds.

16. Provide copies of preliminary construction plans and specifications. Include them as Exhibit O. Final plans will be required prior to disbursement.

EXPORT LOANS

17. Does your business presently engage in Export Trade?
Check here: Yes [No

18. Will you be using proceeds from this loan to support your company's exports?
Check here: Yes [No

19. Would you like information on Exporting?
Check here: Yes   No

AGREEMENTS AND CERTIFICATIONS

Agreements of non-employment of SBA Personnel: I agree that if SBA approves this loan application I will not, for at least two years, hire as an employee or consultant anyone that was employed by SBA during the one year period prior to the disbursement of the loan.

Certification: I certify: (a) I have not paid anyone connected with the Federal Government for help in getting this loan. I also agree to report to the SBA office of the Inspector General, Washington, DC 20416 any Federal Government employee who offers, in return for any type of compensation, to help get this loan approved.

(b) All information in this application and the Exhibits are true and complete to the best of my knowledge and are submitted to SBA so SBA can decide whether to grant a loan or participate with a lending institution in a loan to me. I agree to pay for or reimburse SBA for the cost of any surveys, title or mortgage examinations, appraisals, credit reports, etc., performed by non-SBA personnel provided I have given my consent-

(c) I understand that I need not pay anybody to deal with SBA. I have read and understand SBA Form 159, which explains SBA policy on representatives and their fees.

(d) As consideration for any Management, Technical, and Business Development Assistance that may be provided, I waive all claims against SBA and its consultants.

If you knowingly make a false statement or overvalue a security to obtain a guaranteed loan from SBA, you can be fined up to $10,000 and/or imprisoned for not more than five years under 18 usc 1001; if submitted to a Federally insured institution, under 18 USC 1014 by Imprisonment of not more than twenty years and/or a fine of not more than $1,000,000. I authorize the SBA's Office of Inspector General to request criminal record information about me from criminal justice agencies for the purpose of determining my eligibility for programs authorized by the Small Business Act, as amended.

If Applicant is a proprietor or general partner, sign below:

By: _____

If Applicant is a Corporation, sign below:

_____
Corporate Name and Seal   Date

By: _____
                    Signature of President

Attested by: _____
                    Signature of Corporate Secretary

SUBMIT COMPLETED APPLICATION TO LENDER OF CHOICE

APPLICANT'S CERTIFICATION

By my signature, I certify that I have read and received a copy of the "STATEMENTS REQUIRED BY LAW AND EXECUTIVE ORDER" which was attached to this application. My signature represents my agreement to comply with the approval of my loan request and to comply, whenever applicable, with the hazard insurance, lead-based paint, civil rights or other limitations in this notice.

Each proprietor, each General Partner, each Limited Partner or Stockholder owning 20% or more, each Guarantor and the spouse of each of these must sign. Each person should sign only once.

Business Name: _____

By: _____   _____
      Signature and Title   Date

Guarantors:

_____   _____
Signature and Title   Date

_____   _____
Signature and Title   Date

_____   _____
Signature and Title   Date

_____   _____
Signature and Title   Date

_____   _____
Signature and Title   Date

_____   _____
Signature and Title   Date

_____   _____
Signature and Title   Date

PLEASE READ DETACH AND RETAIN FOR YOUR RECORDS
STATEMENTS REQUIRED BY LAW AND EXECUTIVE ORDER

Federal executive agencies, including the Small Business Administration (SBA), are required to withhold or limit financial assistance, to impose special conditions on approved loans, to provide special notices to applicants or borrowers and to require special reports and data from borrowers in order to comply with legislation passed by the Congress and Executive Orders issued by the President and by the provisions of various inter-agency agreements. SBA has issued regulations and procedures that implement these laws and executive orders, and they are contained in Parts 112, 113, 116, and 117, Title 13, Code of Federal Regulations Chapter 1, or Standard Operating Procedures.

Freedom of Information Act (5 U.S.C. 552)
This law provides, with some exceptions, that SBA must supply information reflected in agency files and records to a person requesting it. Information about approved loans that will be automatically released includes, among other things, statistics on our loan programs (individual borrowers are not identified in the statistics) and other information such as the names of the borrowers (and their officers, directors, stockholders or partners), the collateral pledged to secure the loan, the amount of the loan, its purpose in general terms and the maturity. Proprietary data on a borrower would not routinely be made available to third parties. All requests under this Act are to be addressed to the nearest SBA office and be identified as a Freedom of Information request.

Privacy Act (5 U.S.C. 552a)
Any person can request to see or get copies of any personal information that SBA has in his or her file, when that file is retrievable by individual identifiers, such as name or social security numbers. Requests for information about another party may be denied unless SBA has the written permission of the individual to release the information to the requestor or unless the information is subject to disclosure under the Freedom of Information Act.

Under the provisions of the Privacy Act, you are not required to provide your social security number. Failure to provide your social security number may not affect any right, benefit or privilege to which you are entitled. Disclosures of name and other personal identifiers are, however, required for a benefit, as SBA requires an individual seeking assistance from SBA to provide it with sufficient information for it to make a character determination. In determining whether an individual is of good character, SBA considers the person's integrity, candor, and disposition toward criminal actions. In making loans pursuant to section 7(a)(6) the Small Business Act (the Act), 15 USC §636 (a)(6), SBA is required to have reasonable assurance that the loan is of sound value and will be repaid or that it is in the best interest of the Government to grant the assistance requested. Additionally, SBA is specifically authorized to verify your criminal history, or lack thereof, pursuant to section 7(a)(1)(B), 15 USC §636(a)(1)(B). Further, for all forms of assistance, SBA is authorized to make all investigations necessary to ensure that a person has not engaged in acts that violate or will violate the Act or the Small Business Investment Act, 15 USC §§634(b)(11) and 687b(a). For these purposes, you are asked to voluntarily provide your social security number to assist SBA is making a character determination and to distinguish you from other individuals with the same or similar name or other personal identifier.

When this information indicates a violation or potential violation of law, whether civil, criminal, or administrative in nature, SBA may refer it to the appropriate agency, whether Federal, State, local, or foreign, charged with responsibility for or otherwise involved in investigation, prosecution, enforcement or prevention of such violations. See 56 Fed. Reg. 8020 (1991) for other published routine uses.

Right to Financial Privacy Act of 1978 (12 U.S.C. 3401)
This is notice to you as required by the Right of Financial Privacy Act of 1978, of SBA's access rights to financial records held by financial institutions that are or have been doing business with you or your business, including any financial institutions participating in a loan or loan guarantee. The law provides that SBA shall have a right of access to your financial records in connection with its consideration or administration of assistance to you in the form of a Government loan or loan guaranty agreement. SBA is required to provide a certificate of its compliance with the Act to a financial institution in connection with its first request for access to your financial records, after which no further certification is required for subsequent accesses. The law also provides that SBA's access rights continue for the term of any approved loan or loan guaranty agreement. No further notice to you of SBA's access rights is required during the term of any such agreement.

The law also authorizes SBA to transfer to another Government authority any financial records included in an application for a loan, or concerning an approved loan or loan guarantee, as necessary to process, service or foreclose on a loan or loan guarantee or to collect on a defaulted loan or loan guarantee. No other transfer of your financial records to another Government authority will be permitted by SBA except as required or permitted by law.

Flood Disaster Protection Act (42 U.S.C. 4011)
Regulations have been issued by the Federal Insurance Administration (FIA) and by SBA implementing this Act and its amendments. These regulations prohibit SBA from making certain loans in an FIA designated floodplain unless Federal flood insurance is purchased as a condition of the loan. Failure to maintain the required level of flood insurance makes the applicant ineligible for any future financial assistance from SBA under any program, including disaster assistance.

Executive Orders -- Floodplain Management and Wetland Protection (42 F.R. 26951 and 42 F.R. 26961)

The SBA discourages any settlement in or development of a floodplain or a wetland. This statement is to notify all SBA loan applicants that such actions are hazardous to both life and property and should be avoided. The additional cost of flood preventive construction must be considered in addition to the possible loss of all assets and investments in future floods.

Occupational Safety and Health Act (15 U.S.C. 651 et seq.)

This legislation authorizes the Occupational Safety and Health Administration in the Department of Labor to require businesses to modify facilities and procedures to protect employees or pay penalty fees. In some instances the business can be forced to cease operations or be prevented from starting operations in a new facility. Therefore, in some instances SBA may require additional information from an applicant to determine whether the business will be in compliance with OSHA regulations and allowed to operate its facility after the loan is approved and disbursed. Signing this form as borrower is a certification that the OSA requirements that apply to the borrower's business have been determined and the borrower to the best of its knowledge is in compliance.

Civil Rights Legislation

All businesses receiving SBA financial assistance must agree not to discriminate in any business practice, including employment practices and services to the public, on the basis of categories cited in 13 C.F.R., Parts 112, 113, and 117 of SBA Regulations. This includes making their goods and services available to handicapped clients or customers. All business borrowers will be required to display the "Equal Employment Opportunity Poster" prescribed by SBA.

Equal Credit Opportunity Act (15 U.S.C. 1691)

The Federal Equal Credit Opportunity Act prohibits creditors from discriminating against credit applicants on the basis of race, color, religion, national origin, sex, marital status or age (provided that the applicant has the capacity to enter into a binding contract); because all or part of the applicant's income derives from any public assistance program, or because the applicant has in good faith exercised any right under the Consumer Credit Protection Act. The Federal agency that administers compliance with this law concerning this creditor is the Federal Trade Commission, Equal Credit Opportunity, Washington, D.C. 20580.

Executive Order 11738 -- Environmental Protection (38 F.R. 25161)

The Executive Order charges SBA with administering its loan programs in a manner that will result in effective enforcement of the Clean Air Act, the Federal Water Pollution Act and other environmental protection legislation. SBA must, therefore, impose conditions on some loans. By acknowledging receipt of this form and presenting the application, the principals of all small businesses borrowing $100,000 or more in direct funds stipulate to the following:

1. That any facility used, or to be used, by the subject firm is not cited on the EPA list of Violating Facilities.

2. That subject firm will comply with all the requirements of Section 114 of the Clean Air Act (42 U.S.C. 7414) and Section 308 of the Water Act (33 U.S.C 1318) relating to inspection, monitoring, entry, reports and information, as well as all other requirements specified in Section 114 and Section 308 of the respective Acts, and all regulations and guidelines issued thereunder.

3. That subject firm will notify SBA of the receipt of any communication from the Director of the Environmental Protection Agency indicating that a facility utilized, or to be utilized, by subject firm is under consideration to be listed on the EPA List of Violating Facilities.

Debt Collection Act of 1982 Deficit Reduction Act of 1984 (31 U.S.C. 3701 et seq. and other titles)

These laws require SBA to aggressively collect any loan payments which become delinquent. SBA must obtain your taxpayer identification number when you apply for a loan. If you receive a loan, and do not make payments as they come due, SBA may take one or more of the following actions:

- Report the status of your loan(s) to credit bureaus
- Hire a collection agency to collect your loan
- Offset your income tax refund or other amounts due to you from the Federal Government
- Suspend or debar you or your company from doing business with the Federal Government
- Refer your loan to the Department of Justice or other attorneys for litigation
- Foreclose on collateral or take other action permitted in the loan instruments.

Immigration Reform and Control Act of 1986 (Pub. L. 99-603)

If you are an alien who was in this country illegally since before January 1, 1982, you may have been granted lawful temporary resident status by the United States Immigration and Naturalization Service pursuant to the Immigration Reform and Control Act of 1986 (Pub. L. 99-603). For five years from the date you are granted such status, you are not eligible for financial assistance from the SBA in the form of a loan or guaranty under section 7(a) of the Small Business Act unless you are disabled or a Cuban or Haitian entrant. When you sign this document, you are making the certification that the Immigration Reform and Control Act of 1986 does not apply to you, or if it does apply, more than five years have elapsed since you have been granted lawful temporary resident status pursuant to such 1986 legislation.

Lead-Based Paint Poisoning Prevention Act (42 U.S.C. 4821 et seq.)

Borrowers using SBA funds for the construction or rehabilitation of a residential structure are prohibited from using lead-based paint (as defined in SBA regulations) on all interior surfaces, whether accessible or not, and exterior surfaces, such as stairs, decks, porches, railings, windows and doors, which are readily accessible to children under 7 years of age. A "residential structure" is any home, apartment, hotel, motel, orphanage, boarding school, dormitory, day care center, extended care facility, college or other school housing, hospital, group practice or community facility and all other residential or institutional structures where persons reside.

A. APPLICANT   Please Print Legibly or Type (ALL BLANKS MUST BE COMPLETED, Use "N/A," If Blank is Not Applicable)

Business Name _____

Trade Name (if different) _____

Type: Proprietorship ☐ Partnership ☐ Corporation ☐ LLC ☐ Other ☐ (Specify)

Address (Physical Location) _____

City _____ State _____ County _____ Zip _____

Mailing Address (if different from above) _____

City _____ State _____ County _____ Zip _____

Phone _____ IRS Tax ID # _____

Business Bank _____ Checking Balance $ _____

Nature of Business _____

Date Business Established _____

Date Current Ownership Established _____

Number of employees _____

Number of affiliate(s) employees _____

Total number of employees after Loan _____

Exporter? Yes ☐ No ☐   Pre-Qual? Yes ☐ No ☐

Franchise? Yes ☐ No ☐ Name _____

B. LOAN REQUEST

AMOUNT $_____ Maturity: _____ Purpose: _____

Have you employed anyone to prepare this application? Yes ☐ No ☐ If Yes, how much was paid? $ _____ How much do you owe? $ _____

Name of Packager _____ Packager's Tax ID No. or Social Security No. _____

C. INDEBTEDNESS: Furnish information on ALL BUSINESS debts. (Attach schedule if needed.) Indicate by an (*) items to be paid by loan proceeds.

To Whom Payable	Purpose	Orig. Date	Cur. Bal.	Int. Rate	Maturity Date	Pmt. Amt.	Pmt Frequency	Collateral	Status

D. PRINCIPALS: Submit a separate Section "D" for each principal of the business (including anyone who was a principal within the last six months).

D1 Full Name _____ Phone _____ Social Security Number _____ Title _____

Address _____ City _____ State _____ Zip _____

Date of Birth _____ Place of Birth (City, ST or Foreign Country) _____ U.S. Citizen? Yes ☐ No ☐ If No, Alien reg. # _____

D2 Percentage Owned _____ % Veteran *: Non-Veteran ☐, Vietnam Era Veteran ☐, Other Veteran ☐   Gender *: Female ☐ Male ☐

Race*: Amer. Indian/Alaska Native ☐ Black/Afr.-Amer. ☐ Asian ☐ Native Hawaiian/Pacific Islander ☐ White ☐ Ethnicity* Hisp./Latino ☐ Not Hisp./Latino ☐

*This data is collected for statistical purposes only. It has no bearing on the credit decision. Disclosure is voluntary. One or more boxes for race may be selected.

D3 PERSONAL FINANCIAL STATEMENT: Complete for all principals with 20% or more ownership. (currently and within the last 6 months).

Liquid Assets $ _____ Ownership in Business $ _____ Real Estate $ _____ Assets Other $ _____ Total Assets $ _____

Liabilities Real Estate $ _____ Liabilities Other $ _____ Total Liabilities $ _____ Net Worth (less value of business) $ _____

Annual Sal. from Bus.$ _____ Other Source of Repayment $ _____ Source _____ Residence: Own ☐ Rent ☐ Other ☐ Mthly Housing $ _____

D4 PAST OR PREVIOUS SBA OR OTHER GOVERNMENT FINANCING: All owners, principals, partners, and affiliates must report these debts.

Borrower Name	Name of Agency	Loan No.	Date	Amount	Balance	Status

D5 ELIGIBILITY AND DISCLOSURES: (THESE QUESTIONS MUST BE COMPLETED. Mark "Yes" box or "No" box as appropriate.):

I.   Are you or your business involved in any pending lawsuits? Yes ☐ No ☐ If Yes, provide the details as Exhibit A.

II. Do you or your spouse or any member of your household, or anyone who owns, manages, or directs your business or their spouses or members of their households work for the Small Business Administration, Small Business Advisory Council, SCORE or ACE, any Federal Agency, or the participating lender? Yes ☐ No ☐ If Yes, please provide the name and address of the person and the office where employed. Label this Exhibit B.

III. Affiliates: Do you or the applicant business have any interest in any other business as owner, principal, partner or manager? Yes ☐ No ☐ If Yes, provide details to Lender. (See Applicant Instructions.)

IV. Are you: (a) presently under indictment, on parole or probation, Yes ☐ No ☐ or (b) have ever been charged with or arrested for any criminal offense other than a minor motor vehicle violation (including offenses which have been dismissed, discharged, or knoll prosequi) Yes ☐ No ☐ or (c) convicted, placed on pretrial diversion, or placed on any form of probation including adjudication withheld pending probation for any criminal offense other than a minor vehicle violation? Yes ☐ No ☐ Cleared for Processing: Date _____ By _____ Fingerprints Waive: Date _____ By _____

V.   I have received and read "STATEMENT REQUIRED BY LAW AND EXECUTIVE ORDER".

If you knowingly make a false statement or overvalue a security to obtain a guaranteed loan from SBA you can be fined up to $10,000 and/or imprisoned for not more than five years under 18 U.S.C.1001; if submitted to a Federally insured institution, under 18 USC 1014 by Imprisonment of not more than twenty years and/or a fine of not more than $1,000,000. I authorize the SBA's Office of Inspector General to request criminal record information about me from criminal justice agencies for the purpose of determining my eligibility for programs authorized by the Small Business Act, as amended.

VI.   Signature _____ Date _____

E. SIGNATURE

I authorize SBA/Lender to make inquiries as necessary to verify the accuracy of the statements made and to determine my creditworthiness. I agree that if SBA approves this loan application I will not, for at least two years, hire as an employee or consultant anyone that was employed by the SBA during the one year period prior to the disbursement of the loan. And, I hereby certify that: (1) as consideration for any Management, Technical, and Business Development Assistance that may be provided, I waive all claims against SBA and its consultants, (2) all information contained in this document and any attachments is true and correct to the best of my knowledge.

Print Name _____ Date _____

Signature _____ Title _____

If Corporation, Attested By: _____
Signature of Corporate Secretary

LENDER'S APPLICATION FOR GUARANTEE
Please Print Legibly or Type **(ALL BLANKS MUST BE COMPLETED, Use "N/A," If Blank is Not Applicable)**

LENDER

Name of Lender _____ Business Name _____ Applicant NAICS Code _____

Lender's Address _____ City _____ State _____ Zip _____

Phone _____ Fax _____ 750 Agreement Date _____ Eligible Passive Concern **Yes** ☐ **No** ☐

LOAN TERMS: The following section should be completed exactly as shown in the LowDoc Program Guide.

SBA Guarantee _____ % Loan Amount _____ No. of Mos. to Maturity _____ Payments: P&I ☐ or P+I ☐ $ _____ No. of Mos. Interest Only _____

Initial Interest Rate: ☐ Fixed _____ % ☐ Variable _____ % Initial spread over WSJ Prime _____ % Adjustment Period: Mthly ☐ Qtrly ☐ Other ☐

Life Insurance required? **Yes** ☐ **No** ☐ On Whom? _____ How much $ _____ Stand-by Agreements? **Yes** ☐ **No** ☐ Amount $ _____

If Start-Up or Purchasing of Existing Business, Amount of Applicant Injection**: Cash $ _____ Assets $ _____ Stand-by Debt $ _____ Other $ _____

Equity in home is not considered injection. Provide a breakdown in Lender's Comments if the injection is in the form of assets other than cash.

Use of Proceeds:		Collateral:			Market	Existing Lien(s) *		Collateral
Amount	Purpose	Type	Description		Value	Lien holder	Balance	Value
	Acquire/Renovate Real Property							
	Acquire Fixed Assets, Non-RE							
	Impact Current Assets/Liabilities							
	Refinance SBA Debt							
	Refinance Non-SBA Debt							
	Purchase Existing Business							
	Other: _____							
	Total (Must equal Loan Amount)							

* If use of proceeds if for debt repayment, Lender must retain copies of refinanced notes. If for participant bank, debt refinancing may exceed 25% of total loan amount.

FINANCIAL STATEMENTS: (Balance Sheet and Current Income Statement must be of the same period)

BALANCE SHEET

☐ Pro Forma ☐ Interim ☐ Year End (As of _____)

ASSETS		LIABILITIES	
Cash Equivalent	_____	Notes Payable	_____
Net Trade Rec.	_____	Trade Payable	_____
Inventory	_____	Current LTD	_____
Other Curr. Assets	_____	Other Curr. Liab.	_____
Total Curr. Assets	_____	Total Curr. Liab.	_____
Net Fixed Assets	_____	Long Term Debt	_____
Other Assets	_____	Other Liabilities	_____
Total Assets	_____	Total Liabilities	_____

Tangible Net Worth* _____
*Including Stand-by debt

INCOME STATEMENT

No. of Interim Mos. _____

	Date	Prior FY	Current	Projected
a)	Net Sales/Revenue	_____	_____	_____
b)	Cost of Sales	_____	_____	_____
c)	Gross Profit	_____	_____	_____
d)	Owner Comp/Drawings	_____	_____	_____
e)	Rent (if applicable)	_____	_____	_____
f)	Depreciation/Amortization	_____	_____	_____
g)	Longterm Debt Int. Exp.	_____	_____	_____
h)	General & Other Exp.	_____	_____	_____
i)	Net Income after "d" above			
A)	Cash Flow (f+g+i)	_____	_____	_____
B)	Total TermDebt P & I	_____	_____	_____
	Debt Coverage Ratio (A / B)			

LENDERS COMMENTS: (Management's character, financial strength of the business, and repayment ability, including forecast. Use separate sheet if necessary)

Business Start-Ups and Purchases: Lender **MUST** comment on management qualifications, location, competitive factors and feasibility of business plan.

_____

_____

_____

_____

_____

_____

_____

J. ELIGIBILITY EVALUATION: Refer to program guide. If you have any eligibility questions, please contact to LowDoc Processing Center before submitting an application.

Eligibility Evaluation: To the best of your ability have you determined that the Borrower meets SBA eligibility requirements as outlined in the "LowDoc Program Guide" and the "Eligibility Checklist"? **Yes** ☐ **No** ☐ (Please note, by law, SBA cannot guarantee ineligible loans.)

I submit this application to SBA for approval subject to the terms and conditions outlined above. Without the participation of SBA to the extent applied for we would not be willing to make this loan, and in our opinion the financial assistance applied for is not otherwise available on reasonable terms. I certify that none of the Lender's employees, officers, directors, or substantial stockholders (more than 10%) have financial interest in the applicant. I also certify that our institution has at least 20 qualified commercial loans outstanding demonstrating our significant experience lending to small business concerns.

Lender Officer (Print Name) _____

Signature of Lender Officer _____ Title _____ Date _____

SBA Form 4-L (8-01) Previous Editions are Obsolete

U.S. SMALL BUSINESS ADMINISTRATION
INSTRUCTIONS FOR APPLICANT ON HOW TO COMPLETE THE SBA*LOWDOC* APPLICATION

The following directions provide assistance in completing the SBA*LowDoc* application. Each numbered section in this guide corresponds to the same number on the SBA*LowDoc* application. Please type or print legibly. **SBA*LowDoc* uses a credit scoring system, thus ALL application entries must be completed or use "N/A" if blank does not apply**. If necessary, use separate sheets of paper for additional answers to each section.

SECTION A: APPLICANT

1. Business Name - Legal name of the entity applying for SBA*LowDoc* loan.
2. Trade Name - The operating name, if different from business name.
3. Type - Legal organizational structure of the business.
4. Address - Street address of business.
5. City, State, County, Zip - City, state, county and zip of the business.
6. Mailing Address (if different from street address).
7. Phone - Telephone number, including area code of the business.
8. IRS Tax ID # - The business employer I.D. number assigned by the IRS, or the owner's social security number. Please do not use "**Pending**" on this line.
9. Business Bank - Financial Institution business is currently using for checking and/or loans.
10. Checking Balance - Current amount business has in checking account.
11. Nature of Business - Examples dairy farm, manufacture tires, wholesale shoes, retail toys, lawyer, etc.
12. Date Business Established - The original date the business was started.
13. Date Current Ownership Established - The date of **the most recent change** in ownership. This includes the date that the current owners acquired or purchased this business or the date of any change in the percentages of ownership of the current owners.
14. # of employees - Number of full and part-time employees on payroll for each pay period for the last 12 months averaged by the number of pay periods.
15. # of affiliate(s) employees - Please note that affiliates are defined as businesses that have common ownership, common management, or contractual relationships that give one control over the other. Calculate same as #14.
16. After the Loan - Anticipated number of employees the business will employ within two years from the date of the loan.
17. Exporter - Mark appropriate box if business exports any product or service.
18. Pre-Qual - Mark appropriate box if Pre-Qualification service used.
19. Franchise - Mark appropriate box if business is a franchise.
20. Franchise name - If business is a franchise.

SECTION B: LOAN REQUEST (Total all SBA debt, including this application, and excluding disaster loans, cannot exceed $150,000)

1. Amount - Total amount of loan requested by borrower.
2. Maturity - Number of months or years until loan is to be repaid.
3. Purpose - Briefly explain how the loan will be used.
4. Have you employed anyone to prepare this application? - Check appropriate box, amount paid, name of packager, Social Security number or Tax I.D. number of packager.

SECTION C: INDEBTEDNESS - Please provide the requested information on all business debts. NO personal debts should be listed in these blocks unless said debts were used for business purposes. Add an additional sheet if necessary. Provide the number of scheduled payments in a 12-month period or other terms, if appropriate, to report "Pmt. Frequency".

SECTION D: PRINCIPALS Complete this section for each principal. Section D can be photocopied for this purpose. **Account for 100 percent of ownership. Principal includes:** 1) the owner of a sole proprietorship; 2) each partner of a partnership; 3) each officer, director, and holder of voting stock of a corporation or a limited liability company; 4) any other person, including a hired manager, who has authority to speak for and commit the borrower in the management of the business. Non-owner officers and directors and officers owning less than 20 percent complete only parts 1,4, and 5.

D-1

1. Name - Full legal name.
2. Phone - Home telephone number including the area code.
3. Social Security Number - nine digit numeric.
4. Title - Position held in the business (i.e., President, Partner, etc.).
5. Address - Street, city, state, county, and zip of home address.
6. Date of Birth - Month, day, year.
7. Place of Birth - Where borrower was born, by city and state (or city and Foreign Country).
8. U.S. Citizen? - Check the proper box.
9. If No, Alien reg #. - If borrower is not a citizen, SBA must have the borrower's registration number.

D-2

1. % Owned – The percentage ownership of each owner. (The total of all must equal 100 Percent).
2. Please check appropriate boxes in this section.

D-3 Personal Financial Statement

1. Liquid Assets - Include liquid assets such as checking, savings, money markets, certificate of deposits, bonds, stocks (publicly traded), cash value of life insurance, and marketable securities. **Do not** include individual retirement accounts, and similar assets.
2. Ownership in Business - Value of ownership in the applicant business.
3. Real Estate - Market value of all real estate owned.
4. Assets Other - Any assets not otherwise listed.
5. Total Assets - Total value of all assets in numbers 1, 2, 3 and 4 of this section, D-3.
6. Liabilities Real Estate - Total of all debt/mortgages on real estate owned.
7. Other Liabilities - Total of all debt excluding real estate debt.
8. Total Liabilities - Total of all liabilities in numbers 6 and 7 of this section, D-3.
9. Net Worth - Difference between total assets, number 5, and total liabilities, number 8.
10. Annual Salary - From the applicant business.
11. Other Sources of Repayment - A Lender or SBA may rely upon a source of cash flow other than from operations of the small business borrower for repayment. That source must be available to the principal(s) on a consistent basis in an amount that sufficiently exceeds the individual's personal needs to permit orderly repayment of the loan over a reasonable period of time.
12. Source - Of other Source of Repayment in number 11.
13. Residence Rent/Own/Other - Indicate if current residence is owned, rented, or other (example, live with relatives).
14. Monthly Housing - Monthly mortgage or rent payment of residence.

D-4 - Past or present SBA or Other Government Financing-

1. Please complete for all principals. Financial Institution, Agency, Loan No., Date, Amount, Balance, and Status. (Outstanding, applied for, paid in full, and any other status.)

D-5 -Eligibility and Disclosures (IMPORTANT, only one signature is allowed in this section. <u>**USE SEPARATE SHEET FOR EACH PRINCIPAL**</u>)

Mark appropriate boxes, sign and date.

INSTRUCTIONS FOR LENDER ON HOW TO COMPLETE THE SBA*LOWDOC* APPLICATION

The following directions provide assistance in completing the SBA*LowDoc* application. Each section corresponds to the same section on the LowDoc application. If a particular section or entry is not specified in this guide, special directions are required to complete that entry. You may find it helpful to refer to the LowDoc Program Guide if there are no credit policy questions. If necessary, use separate sheets of paper for additional answers to each section. **ALL BLANKS MUST BE COMPLETED - USE N/A IF "Blank" DOES NOT APPLY**.

SECTION F: LENDER - If you do not have the date of the latest 750 agreement, please call your SBA District/Branch Office and they will provide you with this information. The appropriate SBA District/Branch Office is based on location of business.

1. Name of Lender - Financial Institution.
2. Business Name - Applicant.
3. Applicant NAICS Code - As listed in then North American Industrial Classification System (NAICS).
4. Lender's Address - Address of Financial Institution ****IMPORTANT**** Must be street address, all loans documents are shipped FEDEX. FEDEX will not deliver to a Post Office Box.
5. Telephone - Lender's Telephone Number, including area code.
6. Fax - Lender's Fax Number, including area code.
7. 750 Date - Date of SBA Guaranty Agreement.

SECTION G: LOAN TERMS - Please complete this section as completely and accurately as possible. The Authorization for Loan Guarantee will usually be based on the terms and conditions provided, but SBA reserves the right to amend them. Any changes will be discussed prior to approval by SBA. Accuracy and completeness will expedite loan closings.

1. SBA Guarantee % - Percentage of SBA Guarantee, maximum 85 percent.
2. Loan Amount - Amount Lender has approved.
3. No. of Months to maturity - Loan maturity in months including interest only payments.
4. Payments- Mark the appropriate box if payments are principal and interest or principal plus accrued interest; enter payment. If you are asking for payments other than monthly, please indicate.
5. No. of Months Interest Only - Only if repayment terms have an interest only period.
6. Initial Interest Rate - Interest rate of the loan at closing and whether it will be fixed or variable.
7. Spread - If interest rate is variable, indicate the spread over the Wall Street Journal Prime Rate. If the adjustment period is other than monthly or quarterly, please check "Other" and indicate the frequency.
8. Life Insurance - Are you requiring principal to obtain and in what amount?
9. Standby Agreement - Who will be executing the standby and in what amount?
10. If Start-Up or Purchase of Existing Amount - Indicate nature of the source by entering the amount of the injection by the appropriate category. "Cash" is money reported on a personal financial statement. "Assets" are those assets reported on a personal financial statement. "Stand-by Debt" is any obligation which will be placed on stand-by. "Other" includes gifts, inheritances and other sources not already mentioned.

Use of Proceeds

Amount and Purpose - "Fixed Assets" includes all fixed assets financed other than real estate, such as vehicles, equipment, furniture and fixtures. "Impact Current Assets/Liability" is amount for inventory and working capital. If "Debt Payment applies, enter name and amount in space provided on application. Refinancing of participant bank debt is limited to 25 percent of loan request. "Other" include the balance of assets financed that are not specified elsewhere, such as working capital, goodwill, leasehold improvements. If the purpose of loan is to purchase a business in entirety, use "purchase of business." If only assets of business are being purchased use of proceeds should be itemized by asset category. .

Collateral

1. Type - Enter the code for type of collateral securing loan: RE-real estate, FF-furniture & fixtures, EQP-equipment; or INV-inventory, etc.
2. Description - Briefly describe collateral (e.g., location of real estate, type of equipment, or description of inventory).
3. Market Value - Should be the lender's assessment of the current market value of collateral. (Please note that market value should be based on prudent lending standards and values should be supported by appropriate documentation.)
4. Existing Lien(s) - If collateral is has existing lien(s), enter the lienholder name and balance outstanding on each. (Please note: enter original amount if real estate mortgage/deed of trust is open-ended.)
5. Collateral Value - Should be the lender's assessment of the collateral's liquidation value net of existing lien(s).

SECTION H: FINANCIAL STATEMENTS

Balance Sheet - this section is a summary of the business' balance sheet. If the businesses is a start-up, enter a pro forma balance sheet, after application of loan proceeds. (**Use Pro Forma <u>only</u> if startup**).

1. As of _____ - Date of the most recent fiscal year statements if within the last three months, or the date of the most recent interim statements if not more than 90 days old at the time SGA receives the application if previous fiscal year statements are over tree months old (Note: the date of the Balance Sheet should correspond with the date of the Current Period in the Income Statement section and the date of personal financial statements).
2. Total Current Assets - Should equal the total of Cash Equivalent, Net Trade Receivable, Inventory, and Other Current Assets. Net Trade Receivables means after deduction of receivables which are unlikely to be collected.
3. Total Assets - Must equal the total of Total Current Assets, Net Fixed Assets, and Other Assets.
4. Total Current Liabilities - Should equal the total of Notes, Trade Payables, Current Portion of Long-Term Debt (Current LTD), and Other Current Liabilities.
5. Total Liabilities - Should equal the total of Total Current Liabilities, Long Term Debt, and Other Liabilities.
6. Tangible Net Worth - Net worth after deducting all intangible assets.

Income Statement - This section is a summary of the business' previous, current and projected cash flow statement. If business is a start-up, enter two years of pro forma data in the "Current" and "Projected" columns.

7. Prior FY - For period of last full fiscal year.
8. Current - Must be for the same period as the Balance Sheet Statement.
9. Projected - Over the next 12 months.
10. Rent (if applicable) - Discontinued rent due to purchase of asset(s) with loan proceeds.
11. Cash Flow - Must equal to the total of the Rent (if this expense is being eliminated), Depreciation/Amortization, Annual Interest Expense on Long Term Debt, and Net Income. (In comments, address whether the depreciation is really available for debt service on the basis of when the depreciable asset will need to be replaced.)
12. Term Debt P&I - For the Current period, enter the total of all term debt payments including principal and interest. For the projected period, enter the total of all term debt payments for the 12-month period, include the new SBA*LowDoc* loan.

SECTION I: LENDER COMMENTS - Lender's analysis of applicant's character, management abilities, financial condition of business, and repayment ability. Also any other comments you feel necessary including whether projections are realistic. Business start-ups and purchases must discuss the amount and nature of the injection of the principal(s) into the business. Lender's comments must also address whether the projections are reasonable and attainable on the basis of the applicant's capacity.

SECTION J: ELIGIBILITY - Use the SBA*LowDoc* Eligibility Checklist to assist in making and documenting the determination of the applicant's eligibility. Please keep justification for this determination in applicant's file.

PLEASE READ DETACH AND RETAIN FOR YOUR RECORDS
STATEMENTS REQUIRED BY LAW AND EXECUTIVE ORDER

Federal executive agencies, including the Small Business Administration (SBA), are required to withhold or limit financial assistance, to impose special conditions on approved loans, to provide special notices to applicants or borrowers and to require special reports and data from borrowers in order to comply with legislation passed by the Congress and Executive Orders issued by the President and by the provisions of various inter-agency agreements. SBA has issued regulations and procedures that implement these laws and executive orders, and they are contained in Parts 112, 113, 116, and 117, Title 13, Code of Federal Regulations Chapter 1, or Standard Operating Procedures.

Freedom of Information Act (5 U.S.C. 552)

This law provides, with some exceptions, that SBA must supply information reflected in agency files and records to a person requesting it. Information about approved loans that will be automatically released includes, among other things, statistics on our loan programs (individual borrowers are not identified in the statistics) and other information such as the names of the borrowers (and their officers, directors, stockholders or partners), the collateral pledged to secure the loan, the amount of the loan, its purpose in general terms and the maturity. Proprietary data on a borrower would not routinely be made available to third parties. All requests under this Act are to be addressed to the nearest SBA office and be identified as a Freedom of Information request.

Privacy Act (5 U.S.C. 552a)

Any person can request to see or get copies of any personal information that SBA has in his or her file, when that file is retrievable by individual identifiers, such as name or social security numbers. Requests for information about another party may be denied unless SBA has the written permission of the individual to release the information to the requestor or unless the information is subject to disclosure under the Freedom of Information Act.

Under the provisions of the Privacy Act, you are not required to provide your social security number. Failure to provide your social security number may not affect any right, benefit or privilege to which you are entitled. Disclosures of name and other personal identifiers are, however, required for a benefit, as SBA requires an individual seeking assistance from SBA to provide it with sufficient information for it to make a character determination. In determining whether an individual is of good character, SBA considers the person's integrity, candor, and disposition toward criminal actions. In making loans pursuant to section 7(a)(6) the Small Business Act (the Act), 15 USC §636 (a)(6), SBA is required to have reasonable assurance that the loan is of sound value and will be repaid or that it is in the best interest of the Government to grant the assistance requested. Additionally, SBA is specifically authorized to verify your criminal history, or lack thereof, pursuant to section 7(a)(1)(B), 15 USC §636(a)(1)(B). Further, for all forms of assistance, SBA is authorized to make all investigations necessary to ensure that a person has not engaged in acts that violate or will violate the Act or the Small Business Investment Act, 15 USC §§634(b)(11) and 687b(a). For these purposes, you are asked to voluntarily provide your social security number to assist SBA is making a character determination and to distinguish you from other individuals with the same or similar name or other personal identifier.

When this information indicates a violation or potential violation of law, whether civil, criminal, or administrative in nature, SBA may refer it to the appropriate agency, whether Federal, State, local, or foreign, charged with responsibility for or otherwise involved in investigation, prosecution, enforcement or prevention of such violations. See 56 Fed. Reg. 8020 (1991) for other published routine uses.

Right to Financial Privacy Act of 1978 (12 U.S.C. 3401)

This is notice to you as required by the Right of Financial Privacy Act of 1978, of SBA's access rights to financial records held by financial institutions that are or have been doing business with you or your business, including any financial institutions participating in a loan or loan guarantee. The law provides that SBA shall have a right of access to your financial records in connection with its consideration or administration of assistance to you in the form of a Government loan or loan guaranty agreement. SBA is required to provide a certificate of its compliance with the Act to a financial institution in connection with its first request for access to your financial records, after which no further certification is required for subsequent accesses. The law also provides that SBA's access rights continue for the term of any approved loan or loan guaranty agreement. No further notice to you of SBA's access rights is required during the term of any such agreement.

The law also authorizes SBA to transfer to another Government authority any financial records included in an application for a loan, or concerning an approved loan or loan guarantee, as necessary to process, service or foreclose on a loan or loan guarantee or to collect on a defaulted loan or loan guarantee. No other transfer of your financial records to another Government authority will be permitted by SBA except as required or permitted by law.

Flood Disaster Protection Act (42 U.S.C. 4011)

Regulations have been issued by the Federal Insurance Administration (FIA) and by SBA implementing this Act and its amendments. These regulations prohibit SBA from making certain loans in an FIA designated floodplain unless Federal flood insurance is purchased as a condition of the loan. Failure to maintain the required level of flood insurance makes the applicant ineligible for any future financial assistance from SBA under any program, including disaster assistance.

Executive Orders -- Floodplain Management and Wetland Protection (42 F.R. 26951 and 42 F.R. 26961)

The SBA discourages any settlement in or development of a floodplain or a wetland. This statement is to notify all SBA loan applicants that such actions are hazardous to both life and property and should be avoided. The additional cost of flood preventive construction must be considered in addition to the possible loss of all assets and investments in future floods.

Occupational Safety and Health Act (15 U.S.C. 651 et seq.)

This legislation authorizes the Occupational Safety and Health Administration in the Department of Labor to require businesses to modify facilities and procedures to protect employees or pay penalty fees. In some instances the business can be forced to cease operations or be prevented from starting operations in a new facility. Therefore, in some instances SBA may require additional information from an applicant to determine whether the business will be in compliance with OSHA regulations and allowed to operate its facility after the loan is approved and disbursed. Signing this form as borrower is a certification that the OSA requirements that apply to the borrower's business have been determined and the borrower to the best of its knowledge is in compliance.

Civil Rights Legislation

All businesses receiving SBA financial assistance must agree not to discriminate in any business practice, including employment practices and services to the public, on the basis of categories cited in 13 C.F.R., Parts 112, 113, and 117 of SBA Regulations. This includes making their goods and services available to handicapped clients or customers. All business borrowers will be required to display the "Equal Employment Opportunity Poster" prescribed by SBA.

Equal Credit Opportunity Act (15 U.S.C. 1691)

The Federal Equal Credit Opportunity Act prohibits creditors from discriminating against credit applicants on the basis of race, color, religion, national origin, sex, marital status or age (provided that the applicant has the capacity to enter into a binding contract); because all or part of the applicant's income derives from any public assistance program, or because the applicant has in good faith exercised any right under the Consumer Credit Protection Act. The Federal agency that administers compliance with this law concerning this creditor is the Federal Trade Commission, Equal Credit Opportunity, Washington, D.C. 20580.

Executive Order 11738 -- Environmental Protection (38 F.R. 25161)

The Executive Order charges SBA with administering its loan programs in a manner that will result in effective enforcement of the Clean Air Act, the Federal Water Pollution Act and other environmental protection legislation. SBA must, therefore, impose conditions on some loans. By acknowledging receipt of this form and presenting the application, the principals of all small businesses borrowing $100,000 or more in direct funds stipulate to the following:

1. That any facility used, or to be used, by the subject firm is not cited on the EPA list of Violating Facilities.

2. That subject firm will comply with all the requirements of Section 114 of the Clean Air Act (42 U.S.C. 7414) and Section 308 of the Water Act (33 U.S.C 1318) relating to inspection, monitoring, entry, reports and information, as well as all other requirements specified in Section 114 and Section 308 of the respective Acts, and all regulations and guidelines issued thereunder.

3. That subject firm will notify SBA of the receipt of any communication from the Director of the Environmental Protection Agency indicating that a facility utilized, or to be utilized, by subject firm is under consideration to be listed on the EPA List of Violating Facilities.

Debt Collection Act of 1982 Deficit Reduction Act of 1984 (31 U.S.C. 3701 et seq. and other titles)

These laws require SBA to aggressively collect any loan payments which become delinquent. SBA must obtain your taxpayer identification number when you apply for a loan. If you receive a loan, and do not make payments as they come due, SBA may take one or more of the following actions:

- Report the status of your loan(s) to credit bureaus
- Hire a collection agency to collect your loan
- Offset your income tax refund or other amounts due to you from the Federal Government
- Suspend or debar you or your company from doing business with the Federal Government
- Refer your loan to the Department of Justice or other attorneys for litigation
- Foreclose on collateral or take other action permitted in the loan instruments.

Immigration Reform and Control Act of 1986 (Pub. L. 99-603)

If you are an alien who was in this country illegally since before January 1, 1982, you may have been granted lawful temporary resident status by the United States Immigration and Naturalization Service pursuant to the Immigration Reform and Control Act of 1986 (Pub. L. 99-603). For five years from the date you are granted such status, you are not eligible for financial assistance from the SBA in the form of a loan or guaranty under section 7(a) of the Small Business Act unless you are disabled or a Cuban or Haitian entrant. When you sign this document, you are making the certification that the Immigration Reform and Control Act of 1986 does not apply to you, or if it does apply, more than five years have elapsed since you have been granted lawful temporary resident status pursuant to such 1986 legislation.

Lead-Based Paint Poisoning Prevention Act (42 U.S.C. 4821 et seq.)

Borrowers using SBA funds for the construction or rehabilitation of a residential structure are prohibited from using lead-based paint (as defined in SBA regulations) on all interior surfaces, whether accessible or not, and exterior surfaces, such as stairs, decks, porches, railings, windows and doors, which are readily accessible to children under 7 years of age. A "residential structure" is any home, apartment, hotel, motel, orphanage, boarding school, dormitory, day care center, extended care facility, college or other school housing, hospital, group practice or community facility and all other residential or institutional structures where persons reside.

PERSONAL FINANCIAL STATEMENT

U.S. SMALL BUSINESS ADMINISTRATION

As of _____ , _____

Complete this form for: (1) each proprietor, or (2) each limited partner who owns 20% or more interest and each general partner, or (3) each stockholder owning 20% or more of voting stock, or (4) any person or entity providing a guaranty on the loan.

Name	Business Phone
Residence Address	Residence Phone
City, State, & Zip Code	
Business Name of Applicant/Borrower	

ASSETS (Omit Cents)		LIABILITIES (Omit Cents)	
Cash on hand & in Banks	$_____	Accounts Payable	$_____
Savings Accounts	$_____	Notes Payable to Banks and Others	$_____
IRA or Other Retirement Account	$_____	(Describe in Section 2)	
Accounts & Notes Receivable	$_____	Installment Account (Auto)	$_____
Life Insurance-Cash Surrender Value Only	$_____	Mo. Payments $_____	
(Complete Section 8)		Installment Account (Other)	$_____
Stocks and Bonds	$_____	Mo. Payments $_____	
(Describe in Section 3)		Loan on Life Insurance	$_____
Real Estate	$_____	Mortgages on Real Estate	$_____
(Describe in Section 4)		(Describe in Section 4)	
Automobile-Present Value	$_____	Unpaid Taxes	$_____
Other Personal Property	$_____	(Describe in Section 6)	
(Describe in Section 5)		Other Liabilities	$_____
Other Assets	$_____	(Describe in Section 7)	
(Describe in Section 5)		Total Liabilities	$_____
		Net Worth	$_____
Total	$_____	**Total**	$_____

Section 1. Source of Income		Contingent Liabilities	
Salary	$_____	As Endorser or Co-Maker	$_____
Net Investment Income	$_____	Legal Claims & Judgments	$_____
Real Estate Income	$_____	Provision for Federal Income Tax	$_____
Other Income (Describe below)*	$_____	Other Special Debt	$_____

Description of Other Income in Section 1.

*Alimony or child support payments need not be disclosed in "Other Income" unless it is desired to have such payments counted toward total income.

Section 2. Notes Payable to Banks and Others. (Use attachments if necessary. Each attachment must be identified as a part of this statement and signed.)

Name and Address of Noteholder(s)	Original Balance	Current Balance	Payment Amount	Frequency (monthly,etc.)	How Secured or Endorsed Type of Collateral

Section 3. Stocks and Bonds. (Use attachments if necessary. Each attachment must be identified as a part of this statement and signed).

Number of Shares	Name of Securities	Cost	Market Value Quotation/Exchange	Date of Quotation/Exchange	Total Value

Section 4. Real Estate Owned.
(List each parcel separately. Use attachment if necessary. Each attachment must be identified as a part of this statement and signed.)

	Property A	Property B	Property C
Type of Property			
Address			
Date Purchased			
Original Cost			
Present Market Value			
Name & Address of Mortgage Holder			
Mortgage Account Number			
Mortgage Balance			
Amount of Payment per Month/Year			
Status of Mortgage			

Section 5. Other Personal Property and Other Assets.
(Describe, and if any is pledged as security, state name and address of lien holder, amount of lien, terms of payment and if delinquent, describe delinquency)

Section 6. Unpaid Taxes.
(Describe in detail, as to type, to whom payable, when due, amount, and to what property, if any, a tax lien attaches.)

Section 7. Other Liabilities.
(Describe in detail.)

Section 8. Life Insurance Held.
(Give face amount and cash surrender value of policies - name of insurance company and beneficiaries)

I authorize SBA/Lender to make inquiries as necessary to verify the accuracy of the statements made and to determine my creditworthiness. I certify the above and the statements contained in the attachments are true and accurate as of the stated date(s). These statements are made for the purpose of either obtaining a loan or guaranteeing a loan. I understand FALSE statements may result in forfeiture of benefits and possible prosecution by the U.S. Attorney General (Reference 18 U.S.C. 1001).

Signature: Date: Social Security Number:

Signature: Date: Social Security Number:

PLEASE NOTE: The estimated average burden hours for the completion of this form is 1.5 hours per response. If you have questions or comments concerning this estimate or any other aspect of this information, please contact Chief, Administrative Branch, U.S. Small Business Administration, Washington, D.C. 20416, and Clearance Officer, Paper Reduction Project (3245-0188), Office of Management and Budget, Washington, D.C. 20503. **PLEASE DO NOT SEND FORMS TO OMB.**

U.S. Small Business Administration
Application for Small Business Loan
(Short Form)
(May be used for Participation Loans of $50,000 and under)

OMB Approval No: 3245-0016
Expiration Date: 11/30/04

Applicant				Address	
Name of Business				Tax I.D. No.	
Street Address				Tel. No. (Include A/C)	
City	County	State	Zip	No. of Employees (including subsidiaries and affiliates)	
Type of Business		Date Business Established		At Time of Application	
				If Loan is Approved	
Bank of Business Account and Address				Subsidiaries or Affiliates (Separate from Above)	
Amount Requested	Show how the proceeds are to be used (round to the nearest hundreds)				
Term Requested _____ Yrs.					

The following schedules must be completed and submitted as a part of the loan application. (Applicant's name and address need only be provided once.) ALL SCHEDULES MUST BE SIGNED AND DATED BY THE PERSON SIGNING THIS FORM:

1. Include financial statements of the applicants listed below:
    ALL FINANCIAL STATEMENTS MUST BE SIGNED AND DATED.

    a. For an existing business, submit year-end financial statements, including a balance sheet, income statement and reconciliation of net worth for up to the last three full fiscal years. (Federal tax returns may be substituted for income statements.) Also submit a balance sheet and income statement for the current period (within 90 days of the filing of the application) with a summarization of the aging of accounts receivable and payable. A projection of income and expenses for one year after the proposed loan is helpful and may be requested by SBA.

    b. For a new business, prepare a balance sheet reflecting the assets, liabilities and net worth of the business assuming the loan is approved and disbursed. In addition, provide a projection of income and expenses for one year after the loan is disbursed.

2. List all assets to be pledged as collateral.

    a. For machinery and/or equipment, provide an itemized list that contains identification numbers for all appropriate items.

    b. For real estae include a legal description of the property.

    Collateral lists additionally should contain the year acquired, original cost, present market value, current balance owed, and name of lienholders. Mark this Schedule A. (SBA Form 4, Schedule A, or a computer-generated facsimile, may be used for this purpose.)

3. The following SBA forms must be submitted by each owner (20% or more ownership), partner, or officer:

    a. A current personal financial statement (SBA Form 413 may be used for this purpose),

    b. SBA Form 912, Personal History Statement. (This also may be required of hired managers who have authority to commit the business)

4. Please provide the following information (in the order shown below) for all members of management including owners, partners, officers and directors:

    Name, Social Security Number, Position held, Home Address, Percentage of Ownership (Total 100%), * Date of Entry/Discharge from Military Service, * Race (American Indian or Alaska Native, Asian, Black or African American, Native Hawaiian or Other Pacific Islander, White-Indicate one or more), *Ethnicity (Hispanic or Latino or Not Hispanic or Latino), * Sex (*This data is collected for statistical purposes and has no bearing on the credit decision.)

    In addition, provide a brief description of the educational, technical and business background for all people listed under management. Mark this Schedule B.

5. Please supply the following information (in the order shown below) on all the applicant's short-term and long-term debt. Indicate by an asterisk (*) items to be paid by loan proceeds and give reasons for payments.
    Orig. Date, Orig. Amt ., Lender, Present Bal., Rate of Int., Maturity Date, Monthly Pmt ., Collateral, and Current or Past Due
    (Principal balance shown should agree with the amounts on the latest balance sheet submitted.) Mark this Schedule C.

6. Please submit a signed and dated SBA Form 1624 regarding certification of debarment and suspension.

Note: The estimated burden completing this form is 0.7 hours per response. You will not be required to respond to collection of information unless it displays a currently valid OMB approval number. Comments on the burden should be sent to the U.S. Small Business Administration, Chief, AIB, 409 3rd St., S.W., Washington, D.C. 20416 and Desk Office for Small Business Administration, Office of Management and Budget, New Executive Office Building, room 10202, Washington, D.C. 20503. OMB Approval (3245-0016).
PLEASE DO NOT SEND FORMS TO OMB. SUBMIT COMPLETED APPLICATION TO LENDER OF CHOICE.

SBA Form 4 (8-01) Short Form
This form was electronically produced by Elite Federal Forms, Inc.

Federal Recycling Program   Printed on Recycled Paper

COMPLETE THE FOLLOWING INFORMATION ONLY IF IT APPLIES

7. If you have any co-signers and/or guarantors for this loan, please submit their names, tax identification/social security numbers, addresses and personal or business financial statements, as appropriate. Mark this Schedule D.

8. If you are buying machinery and/or equipment with the loan, you must include a list of the equipment and cost (as quoted by the supplier) and the supplier's name, address and telephone number. Mark this Schedule E

9. If you, your business, or any of the officers of your business are, or have been, involved in pending lawsuits, bankruptcy or insolvency proceedings, provide the details. Mark this Schedule F.

10. If you, your spouse, any member of your household, anyone who owns, manages or directs your business, their spouses, or members of their households work for the Small Business Administration, Small Business Advisory Council, SCORE, ACE, any Federal agency, or the participating lender, please provide the name and address of the person and the office where the person is employed. Mark this Schedule G.

11. If the applicant, its owners, or majority stockholders own or have a controlling interest in other businesses, please provide their names and the relationship with your company along with the most recent year-end financial statements for each affiliate. Mark this Schedule H.

12. If the applicant buys from, sells to, or uses the services of any concern in which someone in your company has a significant financial interest, please provide details. Mark this Schedule I.

13. If the applicant or any principals or affiliates have ever requested previous SBA or other Government financing, please supply the following information: Identify the applicant, name the Government agency, date of request, whether approved or declined, original amount of the loan, present balance, monthly payments, whether current or past due, and purpose of the loan. Mark it Schedule J.

14. If anyone assisted in the preparation of this application other than the applicant, please list the name(s), occupation(s), their address(es), and total fees. Mark this Schedule K.

FRANCHISE LOANS ONLY

15. If the applicant is a franchise, include a copy of the Franchise documents available from the Franchiser(by law). Mark this Schedule L.

FOR CONSTRUCTION AND/OR RENOVATIONS OVER $10,000

16. Include, as a separate schedule, the estimated cost of the project and a statement about the source of any additional funds, other than the loan requested, for this purpose. Mark this Schedule M.

17. Provide copies of preliminary construction plans and specifications. Include them as Schedule N. Final plans will be required prior to disbursement.

EXPORT LOANS ONLY

18. If loan proceeds will be used for exporting, check here _____

SUBMIT COMPLETED APPLICATION TO LENDER OF CHOICE

TO BE COMPLETED BY ALL APPLICANTS AGREEMENTS AND CERTIFICATIONS

Agreement of Non-employment of SBA Personnel: I agree that, if SBA approves this loan application, I will not hire anyone that was employed by SBA during the one-year period prior to the application for the loan as an employee or consultant for at least two years.

Certifications: I certify:

(a) I have not paid anyone connected with the Federal government for help in getting this loan. I also agree to report any Federal government employee who offers to help get this loan approved in return for any type of compensation to the SBA Office of Inspector General, Washington, D.C. 20416.

(b) All information in this application and the schedules is true and complete to the best of **my knowledge and is submitted to SBA** so that SBA can decide whether to participate with a lending institution in a loan to me. I agree to pay for or reimburse SBA for the cost of any surveys, title or mortgage examinations, appraisals, etc., performed by non-SBA personnel provided I have given my consent.

(c) I understand that I need not pay anybody to deal with SBA. I have read and understand Form 159, which explains SBA policy on representatives and their fees.

(d) As consideration for any management, technical, and Business Development Assistance that may be provided, I waive all claims against SBA and its consultants.

(e) I have read and received a copy of the "STATEMENTS REQUIRED BY LAWS AND EXECUTIVE ORDER" which was attached to this application.

If you knowingly make a false statement or overvalue a security to obtain a guaranteed loan from SBA, you can be fined up to $10,000 and/or imprisoned for not more than five years under 18 U.S.C.1001; if submitted to a Federally insured institution, under 18 USC 1014 by imprisonment of not more than twenty years and/or a fine of not more than $1,000,000. I authorize the SBA's Office of

If Applicant is a proprietor or general partner, sign below:

By: _____ Dated: _____

If Applicant is a corporation, sign below:

_____ Dated: _____
Corporate Name and Seal

By: _____ Dated: _____
Signature of President

Attested by: _____ Dated: _____
Signature of Corporate Official

The Proprietor, each General Partner (or Limited Partner owning 20% or more), each Guarantor, each Corporate officer, each Director, each Stockholder owning 20% or more, and, where appropriate, the spouses of each of these must sign. The person signing on behalf of the business must also sign individually.

_____ Dated: _____
Signature

_____ Dated: _____
Signature

PLEASE READ DETACH AND RETAIN FOR YOUR RECORDS
STATEMENTS REQUIRED BY LAW AND EXECUTIVE ORDER

Federal executive agencies, including the Small Business Administration (SBA), are required to withhold or limit financial assistance, to impose special conditions on approved loans, to provide special notices to applicants or borrowers and to require special reports and data from borrowers in order to comply with legislation passed by the Congress and Executive Orders issued by the President and by the provisions of various inter-agency agreements. SBA has issued regulations and procedures that implement these laws and executive orders, and they are contained in Parts 112, 113, 116, and 117, Title 13, Code of Federal Regulations Chapter 1, or Standard Operating Procedures.

Freedom of Information Act (5 U.S.C. 552)

This law provides, with some exceptions, that SBA must supply information reflected in agency files and records to a person requesting it. Information about approved loans that will be automatically released includes, among other things, statistics on our loan programs (individual borrowers are not identified in the statistics) and other information such as the names of the borrowers (and their officers, directors, stockholders or partners), the collateral pledged to secure the loan, the amount of the loan, its purpose in general terms and the maturity. Proprietary data on a borrower would not routinely be made available to third parties. All requests under this Act are to be addressed to the nearest SBA office and be identified as a Freedom of Information request.

Privacy Act (5 U.S.C. 552a)

Any person can request to see or get copies of any personal information that SBA has in his or her file, when that file is retrievable by individual identifiers, such as name or social security numbers. Requests for information about another party may be denied unless SBA has the written permission of the individual to release the information to the requestor or unless the information is subject to disclosure under the Freedom of Information Act.

Under the provisions of the Privacy Act, you are not required to provide your social security number. Failure to provide your social security number may not affect any right, benefit or privilege to which you are entitled. Disclosures of name and other personal identifiers are, however, required for a benefit, as SBA requires an individual seeking assistance from SBA to provide it with sufficient information for it to make a character determination. In determining whether an individual is of good character, SBA considers the person's integrity, candor, and disposition toward criminal actions. In making loans pursuant to section 7(a)(6) the Small Business Act (the Act), 15 USC §636 (a)(6), SBA is required to have reasonable assurance that the loan is of sound value and will be repaid or that it is in the best interest of the Government to grant the assistance requested. Additionally, SBA is specifically authorized to verify your criminal history, or lack thereof, pursuant to section 7(a)(1)(B), 15 USC §636(a)(1)(B). Further, for all forms of assistance, SBA is authorized to make all investigations necessary to ensure that a person has not engaged in acts that violate or will violate the Act or the Small Business Investment Act, 15 USC §§634(b)(11) and 687b(a). For these purposes, you are asked to voluntarily provide your social security number to assist SBA is making a character determination and to distinguish you from other individuals with the same or similar name or other personal identifier.

When this information indicates a violation or potential violation of law, whether civil, criminal, or administrative in nature, SBA may refer it to the appropriate agency, whether Federal, State, local, or foreign, charged with responsibility for or otherwise involved in investigation, prosecution, enforcement or prevention of such violations. See 56 Fed. Reg. 8020 (1991) for other published routine uses.

Right to Financial Privacy Act of 1978 (12 U.S.C. 3401)

This is notice to you as required by the Right of Financial Privacy Act of 1978, of SBA's access rights to financial records held by financial institutions that are or have been doing business with you or your business, including any financial institutions participating in a loan or loan guarantee. The law provides that SBA shall have a right of access to your financial records in connection with its consideration or administration of assistance to you in the form of a Government loan or loan guaranty agreement. SBA is required to provide a certificate of its compliance with the Act to a financial institution in connection with its first request for access to your financial records, after which no further certification is required for subsequent accesses. The law also provides that SBA's access rights continue for the term of any approved loan or loan guaranty agreement. No further notice to you of SBA's access rights is required during the term of any such agreement.

The law also authorizes SBA to transfer to another Government authority any financial records included in an application for a loan, or concerning an approved loan or loan guarantee, as necessary to process, service or foreclose on a loan or loan guarantee or to collect on a defaulted loan or loan guarantee. No other transfer of your financial records to another Government authority will be permitted by SBA except as required or permitted by law.

Flood Disaster Protection Act (42 U.S.C. 4011)

Regulations have been issued by the Federal Insurance Administration (FIA) and by SBA implementing this Act and its amendments. These regulations prohibit SBA from making certain loans in an FIA designated floodplain unless Federal flood insurance is purchased as a condition of the loan. Failure to maintain the required level of flood insurance makes the applicant ineligible for any future financial assistance from SBA under any program, including disaster assistance.

Executive Orders -- Floodplain Management and Wetland Protection (42 F.R. 26951 and 42 F.R. 26961)

The SBA discourages any settlement in or development of a floodplain or a wetland. This statement is to notify all SBA loan applicants that such actions are hazardous to both life and property and should be avoided. The additional cost of flood preventive construction must be considered in addition to the possible loss of all assets and investments in future floods.

Occupational Safety and Health Act (15 U.S.C. 651 et seq.)

This legislation authorizes the Occupational Safety and Health Administration in the Department of Labor to require businesses to modify facilities and procedures to protect employees or pay penalty fees. In some instances the business can be forced to cease operations or be prevented from starting operations in a new facility. Therefore, in some instances SBA may require additional information from an applicant to determine whether the business will be in compliance with OSHA regulations and allowed to operate its facility after the loan is approved and disbursed. Signing this form as borrower is a certification that the OSA requirements that apply to the borrower's business have been determined and the borrower to the best of its knowledge is in compliance.

Civil Rights Legislation

All businesses receiving SBA financial assistance must agree not to discriminate in any business practice, including employment practices and services to the public, on the basis of categories cited in 13 C.F.R., Parts 112, 113, and 117 of SBA Regulations. This includes making their goods and services available to handicapped clients or customers. All business borrowers will be required to display the "Equal Employment Opportunity Poster" prescribed by SBA.

Equal Credit Opportunity Act (15 U.S.C. 1691)

The Federal Equal Credit Opportunity Act prohibits creditors from discriminating against credit applicants on the basis of race, color, religion, national origin, sex, marital status or age (provided that the applicant has the capacity to enter into a binding contract); because all or part of the applicant's income derives from any public assistance program, or because the applicant has in good faith exercised any right under the Consumer Credit Protection Act. The Federal agency that administers compliance with this law concerning this creditor is the Federal Trade Commission, Equal Credit Opportunity, Washington, D.C. 20580.

Executive Order 11738 -- Environmental Protection (38 F.R. 25161)

The Executive Order charges SBA with administering its loan programs in a manner that will result in effective enforcement of the Clean Air Act, the Federal Water Pollution Act and other environmental protection legislation. SBA must, therefore, impose conditions on some loans. By acknowledging receipt of this form and presenting the application, the principals of all small businesses borrowing $100,000 or more in direct funds stipulate to the following:

1. That any facility used, or to be used, by the subject firm is not cited on the EPA list of Violating Facilities.

2. That subject firm will comply with all the requirements of Section 114 of the Clean Air Act (42 U.S.C. 7414) and Section 308 of the Water Act (33 U.S.C 1318) relating to inspection, monitoring, entry, reports and information, as well as all other requirements specified in Section 114 and Section 308 of the respective Acts, and all regulations and guidelines issued thereunder.

3. That subject firm will notify SBA of the receipt of any communication from the Director of the Environmental Protection Agency indicating that a facility utilized, or to be utilized, by subject firm is under consideration to be listed on the EPA List of Violating Facilities.

Debt Collection Act of 1982 Deficit Reduction Act of 1984 (31 U.S.C. 3701 et seq. and other titles)

These laws require SBA to aggressively collect any loan payments which become delinquent. SBA must obtain your taxpayer identification number when you apply for a loan. If you receive a loan, and do not make payments as they come due, SBA may take one or more of the following actions:

- Report the status of your loan(s) to credit bureaus
- Hire a collection agency to collect your loan
- Offset your income tax refund or other amounts due to you from the Federal Government
- Suspend or debar you or your company from doing business with the Federal Government
- Refer your loan to the Department of Justice or other attorneys for litigation
- Foreclose on collateral or take other action permitted in the loan instruments.

Immigration Reform and Control Act of 1986 (Pub. L. 99-603)

If you are an alien who was in this country illegally since before January 1, 1982, you may have been granted lawful temporary resident status by the United States Immigration and Naturalization Service pursuant to the Immigration Reform and Control Act of 1986 (Pub. L. 99-603). For five years from the date you are granted such status, you are not eligible for financial assistance from the SBA in the form of a loan or guaranty under section 7(a) of the Small Business Act unless you are disabled or a Cuban or Haitian entrant. When you sign this document, you are making the certification that the Immigration Reform and Control Act of 1986 does not apply to you, or if it does apply, more than five years have elapsed since you have been granted lawful temporary resident status pursuant to such 1986 legislation.

Lead-Based Paint Poisoning Prevention Act (42 U.S.C. 4821 et seq.)

Borrowers using SBA funds for the construction or rehabilitation of a residential structure are prohibited from using lead-based paint (as defined in SBA regulations) on all interior surfaces, whether accessible or not, and exterior surfaces, such as stairs, decks, porches, railings, windows and doors, which are readily accessible to children under 7 years of age. A "residential structure" is any home, apartment, hotel, motel, orphanage, boarding school, dormitory, day care center, extended care facility, college or other school housing, hospital, group practice or community facility and all other residential or institutional structures where persons reside.

U.S. SMALL BUSINESS ADMINISTRATION
SCHEDULE OF COLLATERAL
Exhibit A

Applicant		
Street Address		
City	**State**	**Zip Code**

LIST ALL COLLATERAL TO BE USED AS SECURITY FOR THIS LOAN

Section I - REAL ESTATE

Attach a copy of the deed(s) containing a full legal description of the land and show the location (street address) and city where the deed(s) is recorded. Following the address below, give a brief description of the improvements, such as size, type of construction, use, number of stories, and present condition (use additional sheet if more space is required).

LIST PARCELS OF REAL ESTATE					
Address	Year Acquired	Original Cost	Market Value	Amount of Lien	Name of Lienholder

Description(s)

SBA Form 4, Schedule A (8-01) Previous Editions Obsolete

This form was electronically produced by Elite Federal Forms, Inc.

Federal Recycling Program   Printed on Recycled Paper

SUBMIT COMPLETED APPLICATION TO LENDER OF CHOICE

SECTION II - PERSONAL PROPERTY

All items listed herein must show manufacturer or make, model, year, and serial number. Items with no serial number must be clearly identified (use additional sheet if more space is required).

Description - Show Manufacturer, Model, Serial No.	Year Acquired	Original Cost	Market Value	Current Lien Balance	Name of Lienholder

All information contained herein is TRUE and CORRECT to the best of my knowldege. **If you knowingly make a false statement or overvalue a security to obtain a guaranteed loan from SBA, you can be fined up to $10,000 and/or imprisoned for not more than five years under 18 usc 1001; if submitted to a Federally Insured Institution, under 18 USC 1014 by Imprisonment of not more than twenty years and/or a fine of not more than $1,000,000.** I authorize the SBA's Office of Inspector General to request criminal record information about me from criminal justice agencies for the purpose of determining my eligibility for programs authorized by the Small Business Act, as amended.

Name _____   Date _____

Name _____   Date _____

NOTE: The estimated burden for completing this form is 2.25 hours per response. You will not be required to respond to collection of information unless it displays a currently valid OMB approval number. Comments on the burden should be sent to U.S. Small Business Administration, Chief, AIB, 409 3rd St., SW, Washington, D.C. 20416 and Desk Officer for Small Business Administration, Office of Management and Budget, New Executive Office Building, Room 10202, Washington, D.C. 20503. **OMB Approval (3245-0016). PLEASE DO NOT SEND FORMS TO OMB.**

SBA Form 4, Schedule A (8-01) Previous Editions Obsolete

OMB APPROVAL NO.3245-01
Expiration Date:9/30/200

United States of America

SMALL BUSINESS ADMINISTRATION

STATEMENT OF PERSONAL HISTORY

Please Read Carefully - Print or Type

Each member of the small business or the development company requesting assistance must submit this form in TRIPLICATE for filing with the SBA application. This form must be filled out and submitted by:

1. By the proprietor, if a sole proprietorship.

2. By each partner, if a partnership.

3. By each officer, director, and additionally by each holder of 20% or more of the ownership stock, if a corporation, limited liability company, or a development company.

Name and Address of Applicant (Firm Name)(Street, City, State, and ZIP Code)

SBA District/Disaster Area Office

Amount Applied for (when applicable) | File No. (if known)

1. Personal Statement of: (State name in full, if no middle name, state (NMN), or if initial only, indicate initial.) List all former names used, and dates each name was used. Use separate sheet if necessary.

First   Middle   Last

Name and Address of participating lender or surety co. (when applicable and known)

2. Date of Birth (Month, day, and year)

3. Place of Birth: (City & State or Foreign Country)

4. Give the percentage of ownership or stock owned or to be owned in the small business or the development company | Social Security No.

U.S. Citizen?   YES   NO
If no, give alien registration number: _____

5. Present residence address:
From:
To:
Address:

Most recent prior address (omit if over 10 years ago):
From:
To:
Address:

Home Telephone No. (Include A/C):

Business Telephone No. (Include A/C):

PLEASE SEE REVERSE SIDE FOR EXPLANATION REGARDING DISCLOSURE OF INFORMATION AND THE USES OF SUCH INFORMATION.

IT IS IMPORTANT THAT THE NEXT THREE QUESTIONS BE ANSWERED COMPLETELY. AN ARREST OR CONVICTION RECORD WILL NOT NECESSARILY DISQUALIFY YOU; HOWEVER, AN UNTRUTHFUL ANSWER WILL CAUSE YOUR APPLICATION TO BE DENIED.

IF YOU ANSWER "YES" TO 6, 7, OR 8, FURNISH DETAILS ON A SEPARATE SHEET. INCLUDE DATES, LOCATION, FINES, SENTENCES, WHETHER MISDEMEANOR OR FELONY, DATES OF PAROLE/PROBATION, UNPAID FINES OR PENALTIES, NAME(S) UNDER WHICH CHARGED, AND ANY OTHER PERTINENT INFORMATION.

6. Are you presently under indictment, on parole or probation?

Yes   No   (If yes, indicate date parole or probation is to expire.)

7. Have you <u>ever</u> been charged with and or arrested for any criminal offense other than a minor motor vehicle violation? Include offenses which have been dismissed, discharged, or not prosecuted (All arrests and charges must be disclosed and explained on an attached sheet.)

Yes   No

8. Have you <u>ever</u> been convicted, placed on pretrial diversion, or placed on any form of probation, including adjudication withheld pending probation, for any criminal offense other than a minor vehicle violation?

Yes   No

9. I authorize the Small Business Administration Office of Inspector General to request criminal record information about me from criminal justice agencies for the purpose of determining my eligibility for programs authorized by the Small Business Act, and the Small Business Investment Act.

<u>CAUTION:</u> Knowingly making a false statement on this form is a violation of Federal law and could result in criminal prosecution, significant civil penalties, and a denial of your loan, surety bond, or other program participation. A false statement is punishable under 18 USC 1001 by imprisonment of not more than five years and/or a fine of not more than $10,000; under 15 USC 645 by imprisonment of not more than two years and/or a fine of not more than $5,000; and, if submitted to a Federally insured institution, under 18 USC 1014 by imprisonment of not more than thirty years and/or a fine of not more than $1,000,000.

Signature | Title | Date

Agency Use Only

10. ☐ Fingerprints Waived _____
       Date   Approving Authority

☐ Fingerprints Required _____
       Date   Approving Authority

Date Sent to OIG _____

11. ☐ Cleared for Processing _____
       Date   Approving Authority

☐ Request a Character Evaluation _____
       Date   Approving Authority

PLEASE NOTE: The estimated burden for completing this form is 15 minutes per response. You are not required to respond to any collection of information unless it displays a currently valid OMB approval number. Comments on the burden should be sent to U.S. Small Business Administration, Chief, AIB, 409 3rd St., S.W., Washington D.C. 20416 and Desk Officer for the Small Business Administration, Office of Management and Budget, New Executive Office Building, Room 10202, Washington, D.C. 20503. OMB Approval 3245-0178. **PLEASE DO NOT SEND FORMS TO OMB.**

SBA 912 (6-00) SOP 5010.4 Previous Edition Obsolete

This form was electronically produced by Elite Federal Forms, Inc.

NOTICES REQUIRED BY LAW

The following is a brief summary of the laws applicable to this solicitation of information.

Paperwork Reduction Act (44 U.S.C. Chapter 35)

SBA is collecting the information on this form to make a character and credit eligibility decision to fund or deny you a loan or other form of assistance. The information is required in order for SBA to have sufficient information to determine whether to provide you with the requested assistance. The information collected may be checked against criminal history indices of the Federal Bureau of Investigation.

Privacy Act (5 U.S.C. § 552a)

Any person can request to see or get copies of any personal information that SBA has in his or her file, when that file is retrievable by individual identifiers, such as name or social security numbers. Requests for information about another party may be denied unless SBA has the written permission of the individual to release the information to the requestor or unless the information is subject to disclosure under the Freedom of Information Act.

Under the provisions of the Privacy Act, you are not required to provide your social security number. Failure to provide your social security number may not affect any right, benefit or privilege to which you are entitled. Disclosures of name and other personal identifiers are, however, required for a benefit, as SBA requires an individual seeking assistance from SBA to provide it with sufficient information for it to make a character determination. In determining whether an individual is of good character, SBA considers the person's integrity, candor, and disposition toward criminal actions. In making loans pursuant to section 7(a)(6) the Small Business Act (the Act), 15 USC § 636 (a)(6), SBA is required to have reasonable assurance that the loan is of sound value and will be repaid or that it is in the best interest of the Government to grant the assistance requested. Additionally, SBA is specifically authorized to verify your criminal history, or lack thereof, pursuant to section 7(a)(1)(B), 15 USC § 636(a)(1)(B). Further, for all forms of assistance, SBA is authorized to make all investigations necessary to ensure that a person has not engaged in acts that violate or will violate the Act or the Small Business Investment Act,15 USC §§ 634(b)(11) and 687b(a). For these purposes, you are asked to voluntarily provide your social security number to assist SBA in making a character determination and to distinguish you from other individuals with the same or similar name or other personal identifier.

When this information indicates a violation or potential violation of law, whether civil, criminal, or administrative in nature, SBA may refer it to the appropriate agency, whether Federal, State, local, or foreign, charged with responsibility for or otherwise involved in investigation, prosecution, enforcement or prevention of such violations. See 56 Fed. Reg. 8020 (1991) for other published routine uses.

INDEX